Arne B

IS UGANDA AN EMERGING ECONOMY?

A report for the OECD project "Emerging Africa"

Nordiska Afrikainstitutet
Uppsala 2001

Indexing terms

Economic performance
Economic policy
Emerging markets
Private sector
Public sector
Structural adjustment

Uganda

Language checking: Elaine Almén

ISSN 1104-8425
ISBN 91-7106-470-2
© the authors and Nordiska Afrikainstitutet 2001
Printed in Sweden by Elanders Digitaltryck AB, Göteborg 2001

Contents

Preface

This report derives from a case study on Uganda within the project Emerging Africa launched by the OECD's Development Centre at the end of 1997. Other cases included Burkina Faso, Côte d'Ivoire, Ghana, Mali, Democratic Republic of the Congo and Tanzania.

The project was embarked upon when Sub-Saharan Africa was showing signs of both economic and political progress in the 1990s. These advances were fragile and uncertain, however, making it difficult to predict how long they would last. The main goal of the Emerging Africa project was thus to access the extent to which Sub-Saharan African countries were capable of sustaining the economic achievements of the 1990s, and whether they would be able to embark upon long-term growth.

This study generally draws on our research on Uganda since the late 1980s, but more specifically on the data, interviews and other material collected in Kampala during two visits in 1998 and 1999. We wish to thank officials in government ministries, the Uganda Investment Authority, Bank of Uganda, Ministry of Finance, The World Bank, East African Development Bank as well as the Office of the Swedish International Development Cooperation Agency (Sida) in Kampala for the assistance rendered.

The study benefited from comments at seminars in Paris, notably from Jean-Claude Berthélemy, the project leader, as well as Ludvig Söderling, Aristomene Varoudakis and other members of the project. The project was financed by generous support from the governments of Switzerland and Belgium. Jean Bonvin, President of the Development Centre until spring 1999, guided the project from the start.

Göteborg, March 2001

Arne Bigsten

Steve Kayizzi-Mugerwa

Acronyms

AIDS	Acquired Immune-Deficiency Syndrome
CG	Consultative Group
COMESA	Common Market for Eastern and Southern Africa
CTL	Commercial Transactions Levy
DAC	Development Assistance Committee
DRC	Direct Resource Cost
ERP	Economic Recovery Programme
EPRC	Economic Policy Research Center
ESAF	Enhanced Structural Adjustment Facility
GDP	Gross Domestic Product
GNP	Gross National Product
HIPC	Highly Indebted Poor Country
IBRD	International Bank for Reconstruction and Development
ICOR	Incremental Capital Output Ratio
IDA	International Development Association
ILO	International Labour Organisation
IGG	Inspector General of Government
IMF	International Monetary Fund
KSE	Kampala Stock Exchange
LDC	Less developed countries
LRA	Lords Resistance Army
MDF	Multilateral Debt Fund
NGO	Non-Governmental Organisation
NPV	Net Present Value
NPART	Non-Performing Assets Restructuring Trust
NRM	National Resistance Movement
OECD	Organisation for Economic Development
OGL	Open General Licensing
PAF	Poverty Action Fund
PEAP	Poverty Eradication Action Plan
PERD	Public Enterprise Reform and Divestiture
PTA	Parents and Teachers Organisation
SIP	Sector Investment Programme
TFP	Total Factor Productivity
UCB	Uganda Commercial Bank
UIA	Uganda Investment Authority
UPE	Universal Primary Education
URA	Uganda Revenue Authority
VAT	Value Added Tax

Introduction

Background

Africa has in the past decade shown a mixed pattern of performance. While control regimes have been abandoned and market-oriented policies adopted in the majority of countries, average growth is still low. This has meant, in turn, that the capacity to address poverty has remained weak. Still, the effort put into the rehabilitation of infrastructure and the reform of institutions in a score of countries has increased optimism for the future, and some countries have seen significant increases in per capita incomes. Sustaining growth will, to a large extent, depend on the success achieved in incorporating the poor into the growth process and the distribution of its benefits. This touches on a variety of issues including asset ownership, access to markets and the poor people's ability to influence policies that affect their lives. Thus to succeed economic reform will have to move in tandem with political reform.

The Development Assistance Committee (DAC) of the OECD has set itself the goal of reducing by half the people living in extreme poverty in the world. This will entail emphasis on universal primary education in all countries, with the view to its achievement by 2015, and the elimination of gender disparities in primary and secondary education. It is also envisaged that the mortality rates for infants and children under 5 will have been reduced by two-thirds by 2005, while a 75 per cent reduction in maternal mortality will have been achieved ten years later. Further, access to reproductive health services and to safe drinking water will have been achieved by 2015.

This study of Uganda is one of half a dozen country investigations undertaken under the OECD Development Centre's project 'Emerging Africa'.[1] The project is motivated by the need to identify "best practices" in Africa's adjustment experience and to help poorer performers to replicate them with the goal of ensuring that African countries are able to reach take-off in the first two decades of the twenty-first century.

It is widely recognised that poverty alleviation in the least developed countries cannot be achieved in the absence of robust economic growth. While historical precedence suggests that even the poorest countries can return to sustainable growth, and eventually "take-off" if the right policies are implemented, this is far from a uniform process (Berthélemy and Varoudakis, 1998). As suggested by the East Asian experience, economic take-off was initially led by a few economies: Japan, South Korea and Taiwan. There are thus leaders as

---

1. Besides Uganda, studied here, the other countries in the project are Côte d'Ivoire, Congo Democratic Republic, Ghana, Tanzania, and Mali.

well as followers. Maximising the chances of success of the current efforts to revive and sustain growth in Africa, such as those implied by the development co-operation strategy of the OECD (DAC, 1996), demands a closer look at those countries where rapid growth already is under way and those likely to achieve it in the medium term. In other words, it is important to identify countries that are on the "right track" in terms of the progress made in the areas of economic and political reform.

Adjustment policies have been tried in many countries in Africa, although only a handful of them have been able to see them through. Thus strong reformers deserve attention because they have been able to create the environment necessary for development assistance to have the best chance of success (Burnside and Dollar, 1997). Good performance has strong demonstration effects, especially since commitment and policy discipline are important ingredients of economic success. However, targeting countries solely on the basis of actions already taken will not by itself provide sufficient incentives to African governments. It must be possible to reward countries for promises of good performance. Moreover, aid is also provided to needy countries, even where an insufficient level of reform work has been undertaken. There is thus need for donor co-ordination with respect to what is demanded of the recipients and in deciding about the prerequisites of sound macroeconomic policy. Thus while individual bilateral donors will continue to emphasise certain issues and target aid according to earlier affiliations, reaching the goals set by the DAC will call for a higher degree of donor policy harmonisation.

Recent research has demonstrated that the growth shortfall of Africa can, to a large extent, be attributed to economic policy failures and to a weak institutional environment (Sachs and Warner, 1997). The main thrust of the analysis will thus focus on the contribution of economic policies to the observed performance in the sample countries. The study looks at issues of macroeconomic stability and economic liberalisation as well as those related to the opening up to foreign trade and investment. Further, issues of governance are crucial to the sustenance of the growth process and need to be reviewed as well.

While the sample countries, with the exception of the Congo Democratic Republic, have had a successful growth performance over the last few years, coupled with an equally good record of economic reform, the continent as a whole has a distinctive record of policy reversal. As a consequence, many of the economic policy reforms that have been reasonably effective elsewhere (especially trade reform) have failed to have the expected results in the case of Africa. This has considerably reduced the region's credibility. The poor regional record raises doubts about the sustainability of reform programmes, even for the currently good performers. Policy credibility and creating good reputations will thus also be focused on. Finally, the study will take into account the social and political factors (political economy) that can ensure the sustainability of reform.

Growth determinants

There are many factors that determine economic growth, not all easily quanti-fiable. As a starting point for our subsequent discussion, let us briefly review the factors that determine income growth in African economies (see also ILO, 1997).

Factor accumulation and technological progress

The accumulation of physical and human capital, efficiency in resource alloca-tion, and acquisition and application of modern technology are the basic de-terminants of growth in any economy. The policy question, which is relevant here, is how the policy environment should be organised in order for it to be able to facilitate the accumulation of production factors, their efficient alloca-tion, as well as the introduction of enhanced technologies. There is now gen-eral agreement that economic policies at the micro level should aim to de-velop and sustain efficient markets, while macro policy must be geared to-wards guaranteeing macroeconomic stability.

Institutions and transaction costs

It has become clear in recent decades, furthermore, that a supportive envi-ronment of efficient institutions is crucial for the functioning of the economy. It is only such institutions that can help lower transaction costs by raising the supply of information and services to economic actors. In most African economies uncertainty is high, thus hindering the expansion of economic transactions and reducing the scope for specialisation. The general uncer-tainty that pervades property rights dissuades economic actors from entering into long-term contracts and thus constrains large investments in fixed capital. This is because given incomplete markets for capital goods, fixed investments might be irreversible and actors want to guard themselves against this even-tuality.

A central question then is what is required for growth-supporting institu-tions to develop? It is not enough to instil the relevant skills in civil servants only to put them into institutions where outsiders determine outcomes. This forces them to become cynical. To avoid this, the norms in government as well as in society at large have to change. A government primarily concerned with its own survival is unlikely to set up the institutions and code of conduct necessary for economic growth. With special interest politics at centre stage, there is bound to be static inefficiency. The latter is bound to make investors cautious, while elsewhere in the economy resources are wasted on rent-seeking activities. However, an open debate can contribute to change and here Uganda is a good example. Recent policy debates indicate a broadening par-ticipation by the population.

Governance and politics

Understanding the nature of the domestic politics is a key to successful economic reform. Many policy interventions in Africa have been discretionary, leading to high level corruption and pervasive rent seeking (Bigsten, 1993; Bigsten and Moene, 1996). A notion that frequently appears in the analyses of the Asian success stories is that of "shared growth". It suggests that in order to participate actively, the mass of the population must see the benefits of growth. However, it is not only the average person who must be included, but also the ruling elite must allow competing groups to benefit, as well as allow new competitors to come in. For shared growth to come about, there is need for a bureaucracy of high quality, which is sufficiently insulated from the various pressure groups. However, it is not easy to create such an institutional set-up without a high degree of political pluralism. Lack of the latter has stifled economic initiatives in many African countries.

Some cross-country evidence

Several cross-country studies of determinants of growth in Africa have been undertaken in recent years. Easterly and Levine (1996) highlight the importance of ethnic fragmentation and the poor quality of infrastructure in their explanation of the poor African performance, while Sachs and Warner (1997) emphasise the role of trade policy and geographical factors. However, looking at the variation of growth within Africa, Rodrik (1998) finds that it is fundamentals such as human capital, fiscal policy, demography and convergence factors that explain intra-country variation and not those of ethnic fragmentation or lack of openness emphasised by others.

An emerging economy

To be able to determine whether African countries are "emerging", it is important to establish some basic characteristics or minimum criteria for an emerging economy. For the purpose of this study, we define an economy as "emerging" if we find that it is in a process of sustainable per capita income growth. We specify a set of criteria or indicators that define whether the growth is sustainable. However, it is not possible to say whether all criteria need to be met or the extent to which they need to be met, but we believe that they can serve as an organising device for our discussion and that on the basis of our evaluation of the pattern of growth we will be able to have a considered opinion on whether Uganda's growth is sufficiently stable to be characterised as long-term sustainable.[2]

---

2. Guillaumont, Guillaumont Jeanneney and Varoudakis (1999) have constructed such a composite indictor for emerging African economies based on a total of fourteen variables, namely five macroeconomic variables (inflation rate, budget deficit as a percentage of GDP, exchange rate premium in the parallel foreign exchange market, a measure of policy induced real effective exchange rate

The criteria we select reflect our reading of the literature partly summarised above, and they can be divided into five sets of indicators. First, an emerging economy would be expected to have a fairly efficient macroeconomic framework accompanied by an appreciable level of international competitiveness. Second, it should be a market economy with reasonably efficient and competitive domestic markets. Third, the level of human resource development as well as that of the quality of infrastructure and institutions would be consistent with the needs of an economy set for rapid expansion. Fourth, a properly functioning economy is partly the result of an adequate level of governance and political accommodation. Last, an emerging economy is expected to become gradually less dependent on aid, relying more on domestic savings and foreign private inflows for investment. Its debt burden also ceases to claim more than a modest share of total resources.

Let us examine these issues in turn. Macroeconomic stability is the foundation of a successful economic policy. It creates confidence among economic actors, thus elongating their planning horizons, and enabling them to invest in large long-term projects that countries with inadequate employment opportunities demand. Low inflation tends to help stabilise the nominal exchange rate as well as the general operation of the financial sector. Long-term financing becomes easier for the business sector, while speculative projects are discouraged. However, while domestic stability helps to alleviate the overvaluation of the exchange rate, on its own this is not enough to ensure increased international competitiveness. To encourage trade expansion supportive policies are needed in the areas of taxation, transport regulation and market access.

Experience also shows that liberalised and competitive domestic markets are essential for efficient resource allocation and thus sustained economic growth. An important component in an enabling economic infrastructure is the financial system. This needs to be stable, diversified, and transparent. It must also be responsive to the needs of the micro-enterprises.

The East Asian experience has shown that countries managed to reach rapid levels of economic growth partly thanks to an earlier emphasis on human capital development and the expansion of primary health care. Studies have shown that inadequate human resources impose a constraint on growth as well as on the country's ability to enter the more lucrative manufacturing niches that have been made possible by global trade. Since many African

misalignment, and degree of the economy's exposure to foreign competition), seven variables of economic performance (growth of per capita GDP, the number of years with positive per capita GDP growth during the last ten years, the number of consecutive years with positive growth during the same period, the number of years with less than 10% inflation and the number of years with higher than 40% inflation during the last ten years, the volatility of inflation, and the investment ratio), and finally two indicators of conflict (the average number of coups and revolution and the average number of external conflicts). Principal component analysis was used to derive weights for the indicators. The indicators for Uganda shows a declining trend between 1970 and 1980, then a short-lived improvement for a few years with a big decline again in 1985–1986, and thereafter sustained improvement up until 1994.

countries have not been able to establish even a system for universal primary education, they will continue to lack adequately trained manpower well into the twenty-first century. Similarly, the poor state of infrastructure implies increased costs for producers, which lowers their competitive edge in international markets. Further, foreign firms will seek to locate in countries or regions where a sufficient level of infrastructure service provision is ensured. An emerging economy would thus have a fairly advanced infrastructure that enables a rapid movement of goods and services at reasonable cost. It would also have developed the capacity to adapt and even develop technology for use at home.

Institutions in Africa were not always intended as enabling structures but rather as vehicles of control and coercion. However, the evolving market structures now demand institutions of a radically different nature. Three functions are envisaged: regulation, service provision and market support. An emerging economy should have an efficient array of institutions or agencies; some run by the private sector to curb the excesses of market actors and to ensure that an acceptable level of competition is upheld. Governance issues have become important in the adjustment debate. It has been argued that governments that fail to clearly demarcate the public and private realms are bound to encourage rent-seeking activities and to regress into patronage with negative implications for efficiency and growth. This is especially crucial in countries where the private sector is still very small, with all the principal actors known to each other, since problems of collusion and insider trading are bound to arise. At the political level, the liberalisation of the economy has raised the number of competing interest groups and the potential for political competition. Much as in the economic sphere, competing political agendas will have to be allowed, and tested in the voters' market. What type of policies are eventually implemented and sustained will depend on the political process. Therefore it may well be that the major growth constraints are to be found in the political sphere. If there is a lot of corruption or political interference in economic activities, growth may come to a halt. Poverty reduction is one of the most important goals of development, but there is also evidence that a sustainable pattern of development requires that a sufficiently broad spectrum of the population is able to share in the growth. Thus, the combination of broad-based growth and poverty reduction has an instrumental value as well.

Finally, an emerging economy would no longer have to rely on aid to meet its resource needs, with resources coming increasingly from domestic savings and foreign risk capital. Furthermore, the debt burden would not be the national concern that it is today for many African countries. Achieving the above would be a significant development since graduation from aid dependency implies that the country has reached a certain degree of maturity, with the credibility of domestic policies no longer singly based on the fulfilment of conditionalities set by external aid agencies. The development agenda would have been "internalised".

On the basis of this set of criteria the rest of this study evaluates economic reforms and performance in Uganda, with a focus on the past decade, in order to determine the extent to which the country can be said to be an emerging economy.

Outline of the study

The study is presented in five parts: part 1 is an overview of the country's long-run economic performance. It looks at developments from the early 1960s, providing a historical account of how the various regimes addressed the economic challenges of their times and how the economy as well as the households responded. Besides a look at the welfare impacts of the policies, this part also highlights various aspects of Uganda's aid dependence. Part II focuses on the macroeconomic policies pursued by the National Resistance Movement (NRM) government since 1986. Three themes are highlighted: the impact of macroeconomic stabilisation on public finance, the evolution of the exchange rate policy, the debt burden and the prospects for debt relief. Part III takes a look at the structural policies directed at long-run growth. The first aspects looked at are those of price and trade reform. Second, the financial system and its challenges are reviewed, including suggestions for making the sector a better tool for resource mobilisation. Third, the state of socio-economic infrastructure is discussed as well as the size and quality of the country's human resources. Part IV looks at public sector management and its implications for the economy. The issues of privatisation, civil service reform, decentralisation, effective regulation, and corporate governance are taken up. Part V concludes the study with a policy discussion.

Part I
An overview of long-run economic performance

I.1. Introduction

Though still a poor country, Uganda was by the end of the 1990s no longer a crisis economy. However, even after a decade of reform-generated growth, per capita incomes are still lower than in 1972. That is at the end of the only other long period of sustainable growth in recent decades. It has yet to put behind it the legacy of the crisis years: political uncertainties, partly owing to wide social and regional gaps, remain, while the country's earlier reputation as a high-risk business environment is not yet eliminated. Still, the recent period of sustained peace has enabled a large portion of the population to be re-incorporated into the market economy and policymakers to embark on wide-ranging social and political reforms.

In Uganda, the four decades since independence have recorded at least as many shifts in policy as there have been regime changes. The nationalist sentiment of the post-independence period led to inward looking policies based on import-substitution, central planning and licensing. This culminated in the concentration of power in the central government and in nationalisation. When Amin took power in the early 1970s, a combination of erratic domestic policies and external shocks led to economic decline. Obote's return to power at the beginning of the 1980s marked a reversal of the earlier emphasis on controls and nationalisation. To encourage foreign investment, market-based policies were re-adopted. However, the regime failed to establish a viable political coalition to ensure longevity. Museveni assumed power in 1986 and his National Resistance Movement (NRM) government has had the longest spate in power of any regime since independence. The period has seen some of the most far-reaching political and economic changes in the country, beginning in 1987 with the launch of an economic reform programme supported by the World Bank and the IMF.

This chapter undertakes an overview of the main policy and institutional features which have characterised the Ugandan economy since the early 1960s, with emphasis on the period of economic reform that began in the second half of the 1980s. The chapter highlights the factors, both endogenous and exogenous, that influenced economic policy. It serves as a general overview of the issues undertaken in the study as a whole.

I.2. Pressures of nationhood, 1960–70

Uganda, as most other African countries, was at independence susceptible to what can be called the "pressures of nationhood". First, there was the need to demonstrate that the new government was capable of rapidly redressing the colonial legacy by improving the provision of education and health services, especially in the countryside, and by creating modern employment in the urban areas. Second, it was felt that the state had to be the main thrust in the economy, implying direct control of the major sectors. Third, the new policy-makers were wary of political competition and discouraged all forms of pluralism, including independent co-operative unions and labour unions. The coercive arm of government, notably the military, was extended. The contradictions inherent in the wish to control national resources, generate growth, remain socially conscious, while at the same time preserving the hold on political power became all too apparent in the latter half of the 1960s.

At independence, the government had adopted a mixed-economy strategy, with private ownership sanctioned by the constitution. Nevertheless the policy thrust of the 1960s was dirigiste. The government believed that assuming a lead in all the major economic activities was the best way of ensuring rapid employment creation and growth. But since Uganda's economy was peasant dominated, with much of the agricultural production done on smallholder holdings, government control of the economy was never pervasive. In retrospect, this was a blessing in disguise: in the chaotic 1970s and 1980s, when the economy was beset by a multitude of setbacks, the bulk of the population could survive on rural production even as the modern sector went into steep decline.

The first national development plan had the goal of raising the standard of living for all Ugandans, with a view to "eliminating poverty" altogether (Uganda, 1965). In a peasant economy, this initially led to policy initiatives towards the agricultural sector, including subsidies on essential agricultural equipment and fertiliser, and the expansion of extension services and research. However, the government's focus soon switched to modern sector employment, which had grown more slowly than expected (see Table I.1). This led in turn to wage legislation, or incomes policy, and the policy of import substitution. The latter was seen as the best means of economic diversification and employment creation (see Elliot, 1973:9). The government thus undertook tariff protection and customs refunds on imported raw materials, while key expatriate personnel were issued temporary work permits on demand (Uganda, 1965). Inherent in the import-substitution strategy was also the wish to catch up with Kenya, which Uganda and Tanzania felt had enjoyed undue advantage as a commercial centre during British rule. Still, at this stage the import-substitution regime was not so rigid as to begin threatening export growth. Exports continued to have large shares in GDP throughout the 1960s.

In the 1960s, an East African Currency Board shared with Kenya and Tanzania controlled what there was of monetary policy. While limiting domestic leeway in the determination of economic policy, it helped keep inflation at bay (see Table I.1). Government simply had no way of financing its deficits by printing money. The Board thus served as what Paul Collier (1994) has called an "external agent of restraint", that is that as a regional organisation it was

resistant to policy swings in individual countries. However, inability to regu-
late domestic credit, especially during the crop-harvest seasons when invariably there was a shortage of working capital, led to vexation. By 1966, Uganda
had established its own central bank.

Table I.1. *Economic performance indicators 1960–70 (indexes:1960=100)*

	1960	1961	1962	1963	1964	1965	1966	1967	1968	1969	1970
GDP growth (%)	3.2	-1.1	4.1	11.7	7.5	0.9	6.3	5.1	3.2	11.7	0.7
GDP per capita index	100	96	96	103	106	102	104	105	104	112	109
Gross domestic investment/GDP (%)	11	10	11	13	12	11	12	13	13	14	13
Gross domestic savings/GDP (%)	16	13	14	17	19	12	12	14	14	15	16
Exports/GDP (%)	26	24	23	27	29	26	26	25	24	21	22
Terms of trade	100	91	91	84	93	85	97	90	94	94	102
Total external debt (million US$)	-	-	-	-	-	-	-	-	-	-	151.7
Formal sector wage employment (index)	100	96.6	94.3	90.8	91.8	98.6	100.6	105.1	115.4	120.8	127.8
Real modern sector wages index	100	110.1	120.0	133.3	144.2	147.1	153.3	153.7	140.2	139.1	136.9
Inflation (GDP deflator)	1	2	-6	7	9	17	-11	5	15	3	2
Growth of money supply (M1) (%)	-	-	-	-	-	-	-	8	21	10	14
Growth of domestic credit (%)	-	-	-	-	-	-	-	-	22	13	23
Growth of credit to government (%)	-	-	-	-	-	-	-	-	35	77	77
Bank deposit interest rate (%)	-	-	-	-	-	-	-	3.5	3.5	3.5	3.5
Population (million)	6.6	6.8	7.1	7.4	7.7	8.0	8.4	8.7	9.1	9.4	9.8

Source: Uganda (1965), Background to the Budget 1965–66; Uganda (1966), Statistical Abstract, 1965;
Uganda (1967), Statistical Abstract 1966; Uganda (various years), Quarterly Economic and Statistical
Bulletin; World Bank (1982); IMF, International Financial Statistics; World Bank: World Develop-
ment Data.

The post-independence decade also saw a rapid expansion of the public sector. The policy of Ugandanisation meant that a number of individuals began
to receive good wages and saw vast improvements in their standards of living. Wage employment, though growing, remained unevenly distributed in
the country as a whole (Bigsten and Kayizzi-Mugerwa, 1992). Kampala had
naturally the largest number of wage employees and, thanks to the government's policy of regional wage differentiation after employees' ability to grow
food, the highest wage levels as well. Real wages grew rapidly in the latter
part of the 1960s (see Ewusi, 1973), although this then lowered the pace of
employment creation initiated by the Second National Development Plan,
1966–71.

In the second half on the 1960s, policymakers were concerned with the
low level of private-sector savings and the slow rate of investment (see Table
I.1). Perhaps not realising that the deteriorating policy environment was the
cause, they blamed the business community, then mainly of Asian origin, for
"sitting on the fence", and for "anti-Uganda" transfers of capital to abroad.
Controls on currency transactions and capital and property transfers were
strengthened. However, the definitive move towards total control came with
the introduction of Obote's Common Man's Charter. By 1970, the state was
then poised to acquire a controlling stake in all the major enterprises in the
country.

The 1960s were characterised by government attempts at responding to the increasingly complex political and economic demands of the post-independence era. Since the challenges of the 1960s were to manifest themselves in various forms in subsequent decades let us summarise them below:

1. how to expand investment and increase economic growth;
2. how to incorporate peasants and the rural sector in the development process;
3. how to redress the inequalities in incomes and opportunities;
4. how to bridge the regional economic gaps;
5. how to preserve political power.

I.3. Policy distortions, external shocks and decline, 1971–80

On taking power in early 1971, Amin reduced state participation in the economy, and the earlier apprehension on the part of the multinationals and the large, mostly Asian owned, companies was temporarily assuaged. However, although Obote was blamed (Uganda, 1972) for "over-concentration on politics, at the expense of taking care of our economic life", the military regime was about to embark on policies that would seriously affect the Uganda economy and the well-being of the people for decades.

From the point of view of the economy, a major negative event was the expulsion of the Ugandan-Asian business families in 1972. Though anti-Asian sentiment was rife in the 1960s, the expulsion was unprecedented. Jamal (1976) has argued that though a long history of economic inequalities between the African majority and the Asians has caused resentment, the expulsion did little to improve income distribution or the welfare of the "common man" in Uganda. In retrospect, the expulsion put an end to Uganda's post-independence prosperity. Investments dried up, exports declined, and per capita incomes fell continuously from 1973 (see Table I.2). Thus, there were three main effects of the Asian expulsion:

1. skilled managers were replaced by largely unskilled people, often drawn from the military and with little education;
2. the appropriation of their properties earned the country a long-lived reputation for lawlessness and property confiscation;
3. the manner in which former Asian businesses were acquired created insecurity of tenure, leading to asset stripping.

Apart from causing the virtual demise of the productive part of the formal sector, another substantial Amin legacy was the expansion of the public sector. Thus while there were only 10 parastatals in 1972, by the mid-1970s there was a total of 23, responsible for up to 250 different business enterprises (Katumba, 1988). However, the managers of the new parastatals lacked both managerial competence and entrepreneurial skill, while the private individuals who had acquired the smaller businesses had soon stripped them of most assets. Moreover, the new parastatals were largely used for state patronage. Thus while they were earlier sources of tax revenue, in the form of corporate taxes, rents, licences and rates (Uganda, 1977:45), they now depended on the government for survival.

Table I.2. *Indicators of economic performance 1972–1980 (indexes:1960=100)*

	1971	1972	1973	1974	1975	1976	1977	1978	1979	1980
GDP growth (%)	-0.2	1	-1	-2	-2	1	-1.6	-5.5	-11	-3.4
GDP per capita (index)	106	104	100	95	90	88	84	77	66	62
Gross domestic investment/GDP (%)	15	11	8	11	8	6	6	8	6	6
Gross domestic savings/GDP (%)	11	13	11	10	5	7	7	3	8	0
Export/GDP (%)	19	18	16	14	8	11	8	4	3	7
Terms of trade (1960=100)	103	94	88	76	78	108	186	119	117	113
Total external debt (million US$)	172.4	177.6	177.4	204.4	211.5	246.5	338.1	449.7	590.2	702.5
Wage employment (index)	132.8	135.0	143.2	150.8	150.5	149.6	150.4	-	-	-
Inflation (GDP deflator)	4	8	24	57	20	46	89	36	216	150
Money supply (M1) (growth %)	2	36	38	43	8	37	30	21	52	31
Domestic credit (growth %)	26	35	37	34	18	27	25	24	23	64
Credit to government (growth %)	64	55	49	35	24	33	15	30	28	59
Interest, bank deposit rate	3.5	3.5	3.5	3.5	3.5	3.5	3.5	3.5	3.5	3.5
Population (million)	10.1	10.3	10.6	10.9	11.2	11.5	11.9	12.3	12.7	13.1

Source: Uganda (various years), Background to the Budget; Uganda (various years), Budget Speech: World Bank: World Development Data.; World Bank (1982).

Thus, economic imbalances emerged early under Amin's regime. Apart from the outcomes of the Asian expulsion, there were also the parallel effects of the oil crisis and the increasing international isolation, which led to loss of aid and commercial credits. However, instead of attempting to correct these shocks via stabilisation policies, the government chose to tighten controls, especially on consumer goods. Sugar was, for example, a sensitive commodity, and since the expulsion of the Asians had reduced production by over 75 per cent, to barely 20,000 tonnes in 1976, the pressure on sugar prices had risen. Licences for dealing in sugar were introduced with stiff penalties for smugglers and other defaulters. For other transactions, import restrictions and exchange controls were introduced as well as a number of new licence requirements. Still, these new regulations had differential impacts on businesses. Influential groups in the military and their allies openly flouted them. Smuggling and black markets became common responses to the substantial rents engendered by the controls.

Close to twenty years after Amin was expelled from Kampala by a combined force of Tanzanian troops and Ugandan rebel groups in 1979, his regime remains an enigma. It had africanised the economy, but had at the same time caused capital flight and the impoverishment of the majority. In the end, Amin's populist agenda failed him. He could not generate the economic resources required to maintain support from the military or to keep the population pacified. The inflation resulting from inadequate policies reduced the value of government salaries, while the level of imports fell in real terms. Thus the resources to support the elite were seriously eroded.

I.4. The slow road to economic reform, 1981–86

The leadership vacuum left by the rapid collapse of Amin's military government increased the level of insecurity, weakening all attempts at economic reform by the three governments that ruled between 1979 and 1980. Thus, coordinated economic reforms were not embarked upon until 1981, when Obote, on his return to power, sought support from the IMF and the World Bank.

The priorities of the Obote II government, as outlined in policy statements, were to raise efficiency in the productive sectors, prudent use of funds and the creation of incentives for both domestic and foreign investors (Uganda, 1981 and 1982). The economy had to become more market oriented. Donor teams including the World Bank and the International Monetary Fund that visited Uganda during this period made similar emphases.

The policies introduced by Obote II in 1981 included:

1. the floating of the Uganda shilling;
2. increased producer prices for export crops;
4. removal of price controls;
5. rationalisation of tax structures;
6. control of government expenditure and increased public sector accountability.

However, the success of the programme hinged on the progress made in the area of exchange rate reform, that is arriving at an exchange rate that would ensure a more efficient resource allocation. However, the reform measures were faced with a degree of resistance and the government had to be cautious, especially with regard to exchange rate liberalisation. Two foreign exchange windows were devised. The rate at window one was set by the Bank of Uganda and was reserved for debt servicing, imports for rehabilitation and payment for traditional exports. The second window was determined by a weekly auction of foreign exchange. While implying a measure of liberalisation, the window system was not favourable to farmers, the main growers of export commodities. When the gap between the windows was at its widest at the beginning of the auction, coffee farmers were indirectly taxed at over 60 per cent. Thus in retrospect, the windows system was an alternative way of taxing poor farmers, especially since exporters of non-traditional goods, mostly richer and capital intensive producers, were allowed to transact at the more favourable rate, window two.

The reforms and the relative peace meant that there was a revival of production and incomes until 1983 (see Table I.3). The government's attempts at reform and the economic recovery were halted in 1984. The guerrilla war, which had erupted after the controversial elections of 1980, subsequently led to a sharp increase in military expenditure. Second, the parliamentary and presidential elections were near. The government was no longer able or willing to keep within the expenditure limits agreed with donors. In 1984 alone there was a fourfold increase in public-sector wages, bank credit to government increased by 70 per cent and money supply increased by 127 per cent. The IMF then withdrew its stand-by programme.

Table I.3. *Economic performance indicators 1981–1986 (index 1960=100)*

	1981	1982	1983	1984	1985	1986
GDP growth (%)	4.0	5.7	7.4	-8.5	2.0	0.3
GDP per capita index (1960=100)	65	67	70	62	61	60
Gross domestic investment/GDP (%)	5	9	7	7	8	8
Gross domestic savings/GDP (%)	0	0	2	6	7	5
Export/GDP (%)	-	9	8	9	9	9
Terms of trade (1960=100)	86	85	88	109	107	122
Total external debt (million US$)	717	882.1	1014.9	1077.4	1238.8	1422.1
Real manufacturing wages (index)	100	108	115	153	135	117
Inflation (GDP deflator)	74	40	22	36	95	96
Money supply (M1) (growth %)	103	5	46	127	140	174
Domestic credit (growth %)	104	35	38	65	114	112
Credit to government (growth %)	109	16	25	70	115	74
Interest, bank deposit rate	5	9	13	18	18	28
Interest, lending rate	6	15	16	24	24	38
Population (million)	13.4	13.8	14.1	14.5	14.8	15.2

Source: Uganda (various years) Background to the Budget; Bank of Uganda (1986), Annual Report 1985; IMF, International Financial Statistics; World Bank (1988), Towards Stabilisation and Economic Recovery; Uganda (1990b) Statistical Bulletin No GDP/2 Gross Domestic Product of Uganda 1981–1989; World Bank: World Development Data.

The period beginning with the collapse of the IMF's stand-by arrangements in mid-1984 to the disintegration of the Military Government in early 1986 marked a steep deterioration in economic performance in Uganda. Foreign exchange controls were tightened in 1985, as arms purchases competed with consumer imports. The looting and general insecurity that accompanied the fall of Obote II in 1985 led to shortages of consumer goods and petrol. The rural economy was devastated. A large part of the coffee harvest was again smuggled out of the country. The economy as a whole then went into a serious downward spiral.

On assuming power in January 1986, the NRM went through an initial period of indecisiveness as it tried to define an economic policy that would attract external support but remain in keeping with its socialist ideas. There was considerable discomfort with the notion of "market forces". State intervention and control were very much part of the general thinking. Three months after assuming power, the new government sought to re-value the currency. There was a strong belief at the time that this would boost the "buying power of the shilling", while also acting as a nominal anchor which would hold down domestic prices (see for instance Malik, 1995). In the wake of continued war expenditures and the need to repair industries and other infrastructure, an artificially strong shilling meant in effect an increase in controls. The government reverted to rationing, based on a priority list of imports including, among others, salt, soap, four brands of petroleum, scholastic materials and agricultural inputs and spares. As an indicator of the priority initially given to foreign exchange allocation, a ministerial committee was set up to supervise it, headed by the Prime Minister. Rent-seeking activities increased, however, impeding recovery.

Thus owing to lack of domestic political stability, the reforms of the first half of the 1980s failed to take root. Governments were too pre-occupied with preserving their hold on power to have given much attention to the detailed work that effective adjustment demands or to taking the necessary steps to attract international capital. It was only when a degree of domestic peace returned towards the end of the 1980s that the reform process was able to begin in earnest.

I.5. From stabilisation to growth: Economic reforms under the NRM, 1987–2000

After a year of policy indecisiveness, the National Resistance Movement made the equivalent of a policy about turn by embarking on an Economic Recovery Programme (ERP) in May 1987, since supported by the World Bank and the IMF. While coverage and emphasis might have evolved with time, the goals of the reform programme remained more or less intact in the following decade: to stabilise the economy, bring about a resumption of growth and enable maintenance of a sustainable balance of payments position. This was to be pegged on public-sector reforms, market and price reforms and exchange rate reforms and trade liberalisation.

However, the first attempt at reform by the NRM failed to bring about stabilisation. In fiscal 1987/88, inflation rose to over 200 per cent, while the balance of payments deteriorated further. The shallow financial system meant that there was a direct relationship between budget deficits and money creation. External shocks worsened the situation, leading to a serious overvaluation of the shilling. The systems created for managing the importation of inputs, notably the Open General Licensing, were affected by lack of local cover (that is lack of a sufficient amount of Uganda shillings to buy foreign exchange). It was apparent, quite early in the scheme, that the OGL system, based on administrative fiat, was supporting inefficient companies and needed to be broadened.

Though the three years that followed the introduction of the ERP in 1987 were rather successful (see Table I.4), with better internal security, increased donor assistance, and expanding agricultural and industrial activities, many problems remained. Export incomes fell as a result of the collapse of coffee prices in the late 1980s, while tight credit policies hampered business expansion. The escalation of military opposition in the North, after a brief lull, forced the government to spend more on defence. The public sector had itself expanded rapidly in the late 1980s. Still, by mid-1989, the economy was well on its way to stabilisation. Growth had been re-established, with a return to positive per capita growth. Inflation was falling and the government was finding other ways of funding its deficit, other than via the traditional expansion of base money. Aid inflows also helped revive production capacities while the first set of economic reforms stabilised the economy.

Table I.4. *Indicators of economic performance 1987–1997 (index and per cent)*

	1987	1988	1989	1990	1991	1992
GDP growth (%)	6.7	7.1	6.4	5.5	5.2	4.5
GDP per capita index (1960=100)	67	70	72	74	75	76
Fixed capital formation/GDP (%)	12	11	11	14	15	15
Gross domestic savings/GDP (%)	0	1	-2	1	1	1
Export/GDP (%)	9	8	7	7	8	7
Terms of trade (1960=100)	72	78	60	47	47	35
Total external debt (million US$)	1940.4	1974.4	2253.5	2668.7	2877.1	3032.0
Real manufacturing wages (1987=100)[1]	100	126	163	194	211	232
Inflation (GDP deflator)	225	164	73	27	32	60
Money supply (M1) (growth %)	167	118	93	40	64	16
Domestic credit (growth %)	116	95	178	58	64	23
Credit to government (growth %)[2]	42	145	-13	42	551	-1
Interest, bank savings rate	23	23	33	32	30	32
Interest, lending rate	30	40	50	36	37	33
Population (million)	15.6	16.0	16.4	16.8	17.2	17.6

	1993	1994	1995	1996	1997	1998	1999
GDP growth (%)	6.3	10.4	8.4	4.7	5.3	7.5	5.0
GDP per capita index (1960=100)	78	84	88	90	92	96	99
Fixed capital formation/GDP (%)	16	14	17	16	16	15	
Gross domestic savings/GDP (%)	2	6	7	4.7			
Export/GDP (%)	8	11	11	15	12		
Terms of trade (1960=100)	42	50	75	60	57	58	
Total external debt (million US$)	3055.5	2999	3387	3513	3606		
Real manufacturing wages (1987=100)[1]	294	405	513				
Inflation (GDP deflator)	1	16	3	5	4	10	5
Money supply (M1) (growth %)	38	37	15				
Domestic credit (growth %)	-6	-1	-13				
Credit to government (growth %)[2]	*	*	*	*	*		
Interest, bank savings rate	12	6	3				
Interest, lending rate	20	22	19				
Population (million)	18.1	18.6	19.2	19.8	20.3	20.9	21.5

[1] Derived from annual wage bill for selected manufacturing industries.
[2] Since the claims of the banking system on government are becoming increasingly negative, it is not meaningful to compute percentage changes 1993–1996.

Sources: Uganda (1996), Background to the Budget 1996/97; Uganda, Key Economic Indicators, January 1996; IMF: International Financial Statistics; World Bank (1995); World Bank Development Data; Statistical Abstract 1998; Bank of Uganda, Monthly Economic Report Jan–March, 1999.

An important step in the liberalisation of the foreign exchange market was taken in 1990, when foreign exchange bureaux were introduced to legalise the black market (Kasekende and Ssemogerere, 1994). The bureaux bought and sold foreign exchange with no questions asked, while the Bank of Uganda was selling foreign exchange in a weekly auction. The gap between the bureaux rate and the official rate was reduced, but it did not disappear due to red tape in the official market as well as the risk of having to pay taxes and duties if trading in that market. To make the official market more efficient a unified interbank foreign exchange market was introduced to replace the auction in 1993. Since then the exchange rate has been driven by market forces, with some mild interventions to reduce swings by the Bank of Uganda.

However, the optimism was short-lived. Following a further weakening of coffee prices and stranded reforms, the government fell back to money printing in the face of a brief aid interruption in early 1991. The reduction in foreign exchange availability led to a sharp depreciation of the shilling at the newly introduced foreign exchange bureaux. Inflation rose rapidly once again, reaching 230 in the first half of 1992.

Quick steps were taken to rectify the macroeconomic setbacks. To focus the policy formulation efforts, the ministries of Finance and Planning and Economic Development were merged. In March 1992, a cash budget system was introduced, with expenditures tied to revenues on a monthly basis. Radically, fourth quarter expenditures for fiscal 1991/92 were slashed by more than 70 per cent across the board. Though this frustrated many donor programmes, it had a favourable impact on the macroeconomic aggregates. Inflation pressure fell, with its annual rate at 10 per cent by May 1992. The exchange rate stabilised at about 1250 to the US dollar. The policymakers had thus skilfully resolved the first real test of their willingness to adhere to the stringent stipulations of the reform. While neighbouring countries had in similar circumstances abandoned the reform programme, Uganda's willingness to persevere won it increased donor support, while at the same time increasing the confidence of policymakers in economic management.

Since the fiscal disruptions of 1992, Uganda has managed to combine high levels of economic growth with low levels of inflation. However, while the first bout of growth was partly ascribed to the recovery of production capacities as peace returned to the country and policies became more predictable (the peace premium), subsequent growth demands investment from both domestic and foreign investors. Aid has provided a crucial cushion since the reforms started, first for the repair of essential infrastructure and second to enable the country to undertake reform measures. In current dollars, Uganda's per capita aid receipts reached 40 US dollars in 1990 and remained high throughout the decade. In terms of GNP, aid flows were close to or over 15 per cent for most of the period. The implied level of aid dependence has worried policymakers. However, it has been argued (see for example White, 1999 and Kayizzi-Mugerwa, 1997) that since African countries are still desperately poor, foreign aid will continue to be a necessary ingredient of their adjustment effort. Aid inflows will be crucial in efforts to compensate the poor and vulnerable groups for the social setbacks before they begin to see improvements.

I.6. Investment and productivity growth

In the previous sections we presented a narrative of the growth record of Uganda. To provide further insights into the determinants of growth we will here first look at the results of a simple growth accounting exercise and then at some data on saving and investment in Uganda.

Berthélemy and Söderling (1998) have investigated periods of high growth in African countries in order to identify the growth determinants. In the case of Uganda they look at the period 1987–1996. They start by estimating a simple production function with constant returns to scale on a panel of 27 African countries using a fixed effect estimator. The dependent variable is labour productivity, and the changes in this are broken down into the contributions of changes in the capital ratio and total factor productivity (TFP), respectively. On the basis of the estimated relation, they then undertake a growth accounting exercise. The results for Uganda are somewhat unusual. It turns out that the capital ratio contributed -7.1 per cent, while TFP contributed 107.1 per cent. The results are similar in the cases of Côte d'Ivoire 1994–1996 and Ghana 1983–1996, two other successful adjusters, while there is a balanced contribution from the two factors for the other cases studied.

Per capita income growth may be caused by either capital accumulation or productivity growth. The reason for the rapid productivity growth in Uganda is probably more due to improved utilisation of existing capacities, made possible by the return of peace and by the gradual reduction in market distortions in, for example, the foreign exchange and labour markets and not new investment. However, if this is true, we must be concerned about the implications for long-term growth, since the effects mentioned are of a one-off character. Without capital deepening Uganda will not be able to diversify its production nor expand its industrial structure. This is necessary if the country is to achieve sustained growth. It is therefore essential to also look at the issues of savings mobilisation and investment behaviour.

Table I.5. *Savings, investment (as % of GDP) and ICOR 1991–1996*

	1991	1992	1993	1994	1995	1996
Gross National Savings/GDP %	2.1	3	3.6	9.3	12.2	12.5
Gross Domestic Savings/ GDP %	0.6	0.4	1.1	4	7.3	6.2
Investment/GDP %	15	15	16	14	17	16
ICOR	2.5	3.1	2.1	1.2	1.6	2.9

Source: Uganda (1998b) and OECD data files. ICOR is defined as investment rate/growth rate.

Gross national savings, that is gross domestic savings plus net income and net current transfers from abroad, have increased in the past decade from 2.1 per cent of GDP in 1991 to 12.5 per cent in 1996 (Table I.5). However, this is more indicative of the rapid increase in net current transfers from abroad than increases in gross domestic savings. Though an improvement from the 1980s, when they were negative, gross domestic savings were still only about 7 per cent of GDP by the mid-1990s. This low level of saving is also reflected in the fact that domestic consumption was larger than GDP up to 1996/97 (Uganda, 1998b). Thus, without foreign aid and capital inflows higher investment would have meant a sharper trade-off between consumption and savings.

Investments, at 16 per cent of GDP in 1996 (with the figure for 1997 estimated at 17 per cent by the Ministry of Finance), are low even by Sub-Saharan African comparison. Private investment, however, has edged upwards from 9.9 per cent in 1993/94 to 11.5 per cent in 1996/97 (Uganda, 1998b), which suggests that the private sector has been responding reasonably well to the stability of the economy and the improved incentives. It is noteworthy, though, that the overwhelming share of investment, 13.5 per cent of GDP in 1996/97, was in construction, while only 3.8 per cent was in machinery and vehicles.[3] This concentration is worrying, since the choice of investing in housing rather than machinery may be an indication that investors are still uncertain about the long-term stability of the business environment. When the economic situation is considered to be risky, structures are a preferred investment object, since the returns on them are less susceptible to the risk of negative changes in the business environment. They are also easier to sell off, in case the investor wants to withdraw from the economy, or to convert to other use. Table I.5 also provides estimates of the incremental capital output ratio (ICOR) for the period 1991–96. The average ICOR for the 1990s is about 2.2, which indicates that capital productivity is high. This to some extent reflects catching-up and increases in capacity utilisation, but also suggests that Uganda was a good environment for investment in the 1990s.

To get access to the tax benefits under the new investment code a firm needs to obtain a licence from the Uganda Investment Authority. The planned investments under the licences issued between 1991 and June 1998 comprised 38 per cent joint ventures, 35 per cent foreign investors and 27 per cent local investors (see Appendix B). The most targeted sector was manufacturing with 39 per cent of all planned investment meant for the sector. Britain was the biggest single foreign investor during the period during the 1990s, followed by Kenya and India. However, many of the investors coming from abroad are Indian entrepreneurs that were active in Uganda before Amin expelled them in the early 1970s.

In July 1997, the old tax-holiday regime was replaced by a new one allowing urban investors to write off 50 per cent of their investment for tax purposes in the first year and rural investors 75 per cent. However, although real estate development does not get the same investment incentives as other areas, there does not seem to be a lack of real estate investment in Kampala or towns in the south of the country.

As an investment promotion agency, the Uganda Investment Authority has tended to interest itself in a variety of areas, thus diluting its effort. It now plans to concentrate its promotion on a smaller number of sectors, especially

---

3. The construction sector has grown rapidly, increasing its share of GDP from 5 to 8 per cent during the last ten years (see Tables A1 and A2 in Appendix A).

those with an export orientation, capable of adding value to output and with backward and employment-generating linkages.

A survey of 1,000 newly established firms undertaken by the UIA (1997), covering the period 1991–96, revealed that actual employment for the sample at 79,970 was slightly higher than the planned 77,983. Notably, employment in agricultural and related projects was close to 75 per cent higher than planned, while for most other sectors the actual outcomes were lower than planned. Moreover, on the whole the investment rates were much lower than planned, with the conversion rate of planned investment into actual investment at about 50 per cent, implying that planned investment (see Appendix B) far exceeded that actually realised.

Table I.6. *Location of new investments in Uganda made during 1991–96*

District	Number of Projects	%
Kampala	769	73.1
Jinja	46	4.4
Mbarara	41	3.9
Mukono	24	2.3
Mbale	21	2.0
Kabale	18	1.7
Masaka	17	1.6
Mpigi	16	1.5
Entebbe/Tororo	13	1.2
Lira	11	1.0

Source: UIA: Investor Survey Report (1997).

The survey also looked at the distribution of new investment projects in the country, as outlined in Table I.6. The table shows that the new investments have been heavily concentrated in Kampala, with a total of 73.1 per cent, while Jinja, the traditional industrial town, only got about 4 per cent of total investments. The shares of the other districts are much smaller still. However, a number of districts, especially in the north, do not appear at all. Thus one of UIA's goals, that of ensuring a more even distribution of economic activity, via investment, has not been met. Still, what is happening is very much a result of the dynamics of agglomeration, with new investors wishing to establish themselves where other firms have already been successful. The steady improvement of infrastructure and services in Kampala and proximity to markets makes it a popular investment destination. This has of course started to create real problems for the planning activities of the UIA, especially with respect to finding new land around Kampala on which to establish new industries. Over the protests of the domestic green lobby, a forest near Kampala was recently allocated to the UIA by the government to expedite the construction of infrastructure for the new investment projects.

In concluding remarks to its survey results, the UIA argues that it might be necessary to refine its own methods of monitoring new firms in order to better understand their intentions, especially with respect to actual investment and employment. However, it is difficult to see how investors can be influenced once in place. Few investors can be expected to stick to their earlier promises in the event of sudden shifts in the economic risks they perceive, especially after knowing the country better, or a changed economic situation due to policy or external shocks not earlier factored into their calculations. However, the UIA could do a better job of increasing investment in other parts of the country, especially the north, where investments have been few and far between in the past decades. In this regard, the UIA plans in the future to emphasise the promotion role more than that of licensing.

I.7. Changes in poverty 1992–1996

Uganda has grown rapidly during the 1990s, but one of the questions being asked is who the beneficiaries have been and the extent to which the country has been able to reduce poverty. The most comprehensive study undertaken so far on the matter is that of Appleton (1998), who uses surveys undertaken by the government covering the period 1992 to 1996 (see also Okurut, Odwee and Adebua, 1998, on regional poverty). He has made a series of adjustments to the data sets to ensure comparability over time, with final estimates, at constant prices, adjusted for regional price differences (Table I.7). It is clear that in both urban and rural areas of Uganda, average real consumption increased over the period 1992 to 1996.

Table I.7. *Adjusted consumption per capita (Ushs per month at 1989 Ushs)*

	1992	1993/94	1994/95	1995/96
Rural	4718	4996	5276	5449
Urban	10470	11709	11793	11924
Total	5438	5833	6096	6353
% on food	58.6	56.6	54.7	52,7

Source: Appleton (1998).

Table I.7 shows that per capita consumption increased by 17 per cent between 1992 and 1995/96, which must be considered rapid. That living standards were improving is also indicated by the fact that the share that households were spending on food declined over the four years. These results can be compared with the national accounts' estimates of private per capita consumption given in Table I.8.

Table I.8. *National accounts estimates of private per capita consumption*

Fiscal year	Real (1989 prices)	% growth
1989/90	5955	3.2
1990/91	6158	3.4
1991/92	6238	1.3
1992/93	6478	3.9
1993/94	6401	-1.2
1994/95	7029	9.8
1995/96	7320	4.1

Source: Estimates from national accounts by Appleton (1998).

The national accounts thus provide estimates of consumption increases of approximately the same magnitude as the household budget surveys. One may thus be fairly certain that real consumption standards have increased.

Appleton then goes on to define a poverty line based on consumption requirements, allowing for regional price differentials and differences in the non-food share for poor households in the various regions. The head count ratios derived from the different surveys are shown in Table I.9.

Table I.9. *Head count poverty ratio (per cent of population below the poverty line) by region*

	1992	1993/94	1994/95	1995/96
National	55.6	50.3	49.2	45.5
Rural	59.4	54.8	53.3	49.7
Urban	29.4	19.6	21.0	20.0
Central	44.7	33.4	29.7	28.0
East	59.5	55.6	64.2	53.3
West	52.5	54.3	48.1	42.3
North	71.4	66.1	62.6	65.1
Central rural	52.9	40.6	35.7	34.4
Central urban	21.2	13.1	11.9	13.6
East rural	61.2	57.9	66.2	55.0
East urban	42.6	28.0	39.7	30.3
West rural	53.6	56.1	49.6	44.1
West urban	34.4	22.5	25.2	13.9
North rural	72.7	68.7	64.3	67.9
North urban	49.7	40.5	41.7	42.8

Source: Appleton (1998).

We see from Table I.9 that poverty has declined over the period not only in the urban areas but in the rural areas as well. Still at an average of 45.5 per cent and reaching 68 per cent in some areas, poverty remains high in Uganda and particularly so in the North and East. That poverty in the North is high is not surprising given the persistence of civil strife in the area and it cannot be successfully addressed until peace returns.

We can also look at the changes in consumption standards over time by decile (Table I.10).

Table I.10. *Mean consumption per adult equivalent by decile in 1989 Ushs (national)*

Decile	1992	1993/94	1994/95	1995/96
1	1422	1735	1748	1645
2	2151	2532	2545	2539
3	2704	3035	3132	3219
4	3263	3578	3671	3750
5	3847	4131	4160	4417
6	4475	4840	4858	5115
7	5255	5608	5645	6091
8	6339	6828	6828	7402
9	8152	8722	8980	9696
10	16736	17283	19365	19614
Total	5438	5833	6096	6353

Source: Appleton (1998).

A disturbing observation is that during the last three years there was no improvement for the bottom quintile, indicating that the poorest groups are not taking part in the growth expansion, while those higher up in the income scale saw considerable improvement. As can be seen in Table I.11, the Gini-coefficient for Uganda remained unchanged between the first and last periods. It is thus obvious that the reduction in poverty in Uganda has been a result of rapid growth, not improved income distribution.

Table I.11. *Gini-coefficients for Uganda*

	Rural	Urban	Total
1992	0.334	0.435	0.380
1993/94	0.305	0.385	0.358
1994/95	0.329	0.414	0.375
1995/96	0.338	0.400	0.379

Source: Appleton (1998).

To get a feel for what has brought about these changes, one can also look at the extent of poverty by sector (defined according to the main activity of the head of household) (Table I.12).

Table I.12. *Poverty (head count) by sector of household head*

Sector	1992	Contribution	1995/96	Contribution
National	55.6	100	45.6	100
Food crop	64.1	54.4	58.3	56.5
Cash crop	59.6	25.2	40.5	24.1
Non-crop agric	51.7	2.4	41.0	1.8
Mining	43.4	0.1	74.2	0.3
Manufacturing	46.3	3.0	27.9	2.1
Public utilities	43.3	0.1	10.9	0.0
Construction	38.3	0.9	34.6	0.8
Trade	26.4	3.2	16.7	2.5
Hotels	26.6	0.3	17.0	0.4
Transportation	31.9	0.8	14.3	0.6
Misc. services	27.7	0.8	26.9	1.3
Gov. services	33.5	4.1	26.2	3.2
Not working	59.8	4.6	62.1	6.6

Source: Appleton (1998).

We see from Table I.12 that crop agriculture makes up 80 per cent of poverty in Uganda. An interesting change between 1992 and 1995/96 is that while food crop producers have only seen modest improvements, their headcount ratio fell from 64.1 per cent to 56.3 per cent, cash crop farmers have gained a lot, and their headcount ratio fell from 59.6 per cent to 41 per cent, partly a result of the coffee boom.

In response to the poverty challenge, the government launched a Poverty Eradication Action Plan (PEAP) in late 1996, although it did not take final shape until 1997. The goal of PEAP is to guide all future public investment and to empower the poor by enhancing their incomes. Among its main strategies is the consolidation of macroeconomic policy in order to maintain the growth momentum. Growth will have to become more broad-based, encompassing the poor and increasing employment opportunities, particularly in agriculture, while increasing the provision of basic social services (Uganda, 1997e, f). It also emphasises the need for the expansion of the private sector and the creation of national capacities to respond to national disasters. Among the priorities of PEAP are primary education, primary healthcare, agricultural extension services, and rural feeder roads. However, Museveni has let it be known that even the military should be on the list since it is crucial to the maintenance of peace. Recently the government also set up a Poverty Action Fund (PAF) to which donors contribute directly. The funds released by the HIPC initiative are also targeted for the PAF. The plan represents a consolidation and extension of government policies in this area, but it is too early to say what the impact will be. However, a meeting in early 1999 between PAF donors and government officials revealed a low level of planning and inadequate vision.

I.8. Aid dependence

Foreign aid has been important for development in Uganda, as indeed for other developing countries. In the past decade, however, concerns have arisen with regard to the lack of aid effectiveness and the problem of aid dependence, as countries fail to embark on sustainable development (Elbadawi, 1998). In this section, we briefly review the aid dependence debate and then look at Uganda's recent experience with aid.

The debate

The post-colonial aid regime was based on a conception of the development process as one where the LDCs were trapped in a low-level equilibrium unable to generate sufficient investment resources to break out of it (see van de Walle, 1998). Aid was considered necessary because international capital markets were imperfect and domestic saving insufficient. The inflow of aid would make it possible to increase the growth rate and lead to take-off into sustained growth. Aid was seen as a temporary gap-filling measure and aid relationships became mainly a government to government transfer activity, with donors retaining the final say in matters of its allocation among activities, although fungibility made the effectiveness of this somewhat illusory.

The management of aid was plagued by various problems and donors became increasingly concerned about its ineffectiveness. During the 1980s structural adjustment policies were introduced and there was a corresponding increase in programme aid. The deepening fiscal crisis among aid recipients made aid management ineffective, and there was little attention paid to the need for long-term institution building. Much aid was now designed to back up the adjustment efforts. It could be, for example, measures to rehabilitate poorly functioning parastatals, or those to alleviate the impact of adjustment. Regular aid also continued, but donors more and more took over functions that traditionally had been in the realm of the government (see Mutalemwa, Noni and Wangwe, 1998).

In the 1990s, the adjustment regime has gradually fallen apart. Overall, aid flows seem to be declining while the increasing emphasis on debt forgiveness may only be just part of an exit strategy. There are suggestions that aid should be given more selectively, and that conditionality should be changed to ex post checks on compliance. However, the idea of giving aid to only efficient recipients may be incompatible with the humanitarian motive and the desire to help the poorest. Still, there will be areas where private investors will not want to enter such as poverty alleviation, human capital development and better governance. To tackle those, NGOs are assuming a larger role as donors attempt to bypass ineffective governments. However, there is also a sustainability problem with NGO aid. It tends to rely almost completely on northern money, and once this is cut off projects often cease to operate. Thus with the goal of more sustainable outcomes, the facilitation of private investment has been added to the general aims of aid in recent years.

There has been some revival of the earlier planning notion now in the form of Sector Investment Programmes (SIPs), based on a sector strategy established by the government and where the donors provide some of the financial resources. However, since aid organisations need to report back to home constituencies on the use of the aid money, they tend to have a preference for concrete projects, but of limited scope. Although donors are often unwilling to let go of their control, SIPs could help enhance government ownership.

There is now among donors increasing emphasis on institution building, which may pave the way towards increased recipient control and better planning. In spite of increasing concerns, reforms of the aid relationship have been slow to be implemented. However, if the reform momentum is to be sustained the debate has to be carried forward by recipients, notably Africa itself.

The case of Uganda

As noted above, Uganda had embarked on economic reform in the second half of the 1980s from a position of serious economic weakness. The country had just gone through close to a decade of civil disturbances and war, the infrastructure was badly damaged, while the social services, education and health especially, had been badly disrupted, and were close to non-existent in the countryside. There was an extreme dearth of resources throughout the country.

The donor community responded positively to the NRM's wish to reform the economy and to introduce a higher level of discipline in the public sector. The initial flow of resources had been of an emergency nature, meant to ensure a rapid rehabilitation of the most essential structures in order to enable the provision of at least some minimum level of basic services. Soon after, however, with policymakers embarking on fully-fledged economic rehabilitation more aid came in.

Table I.13 provides some indicators of Uganda's aid dependence from the mid-1970s. Since donors had quit Uganda en masse in the 1970s, little aid came into the country in that decade. In 1978 when the battle to expel Amin was embarked on, aid comprised a mere 3 per cent of central government expenditure, or 3.5 per cent of the value of imports. Aid per capita was then only 1.5 dollars. The return of Obote to power in the 1980s saw a reversal of the aid trends, with large increases in the early 1980s. It was estimated, for example, that aid at this time was equivalent to 148 per cent of gross domestic investment and close to 10 per cent of GNP.

Table I.13. *Measures of aid dependence*

	% of central government expenditures	% of GNP	% of gross domestic investment	% of imports of goods and services	Aid per capita (current US$)
1975	10.7	..	..	15.0	4.3
1976	4.8	..	..	7.5	1.9
1977	3.0	..	..	3.5	1.5
1978	4.6	..	..	7.5	2.9
1979	5.7	..	..	12.0	3.7
1980	11.0	9.2	148.4	25.3	8.9
1981	53.2	13.7	180.9	34.6	10.4
1982	29.9	8.2	67.0	25.3	9.9
1983	31.6	8.2	82.3	25.2	10.0
1984	50.8	4.6	55.7	32.7	11.7
1985	52.6	5.2	58.6	33.5	12.7
1986	60.5	5.1	59.6	40.3	13.7
1987	..	4.5	45.9	43.3	18.9
1988	..	5.6	51.7	49.2	23.8
1989	..	7.8	69.0	51.8	25.6
1990	..	15.9	122.7	89.1	41.1
1991	..	20.4	132.3	91.1	39.5
1992	..	26.3	159.9	108.4	41.7
1993	..	19.3	124.7	81.4	34.0
1994	..	19.1	128.9	82.6	40.5
1995	..	14.6	89.5	56.9	43.3
1996	..	11.3	68.3	41.0	34.6

Source: World Bank, World Development Data 1998.

Beginning with the late 1980s, aid inflows have increased rapidly. In 1991, for example, aid inflows were the equivalent of 20 per cent of GNP, over 100 per cent the value of exports of goods and services. Aid per capita in current dollars had risen to 41.7. By then the dangers of aid dependence, including the implications of a rising debt burden were frequently voiced. For a poor country, still ravaged by civil war, some of the conditionalities imposed, especially on public sector expenditures, seemed excessive. Similar demands were rejected by other African countries. In retrospect, the conditionalities helped impose a level of discipline on the public sector and the bureaucracy at a time of a general shortage of managerial and technical resources.

However, increasing aid dependence brought with it a number of problems. First, the proliferation of projects tends to overwhelm the management resources of an inadequately staffed and poorly remunerated civil service.

This might entice government officers to engage in rent-seeking activities. However, increased donor money also tends to distort the remuneration structures of central government as donors try to enhance the efficiency of their projects by increasing wages via a number of allowances. In a study of economic reform in Uganda, Bigsten and Kayizzi-Mugerwa (1992) were able to count up to 10 different wage- enhancing techniques used by the donor community. These included travel allowances, food baskets, responsibility allowances, and hardship allowances. While donors wish to improve their effectiveness via these measures, there are serious implications for future attempts at wage harmonisation. Indeed in spite of a huge underemployed population, Uganda is considered in the region to be a high cost economy, partly as a result of the aid inflows. This is also related to the appreciation of the exchange rate, which hurts exports, in Uganda that of the traditional crops coffee, tea and tobacco.

As government was overwhelmed by the aid inflows and projects failed to be properly implemented, donors have sought to reach out to the non-governmental organisations (NGOs). The latter have mushroomed in the past decade, and now cover most aspects of the economy and social life. It has been said that this refocusing of the means of intervention has had some positive impact, especially in the countryside. NGOs are able to operate closely with the recipients and encourage a participatory approach to development. This has seemed to fit with the government's decentralisation plans. However, they have been criticised for introducing too many small agendas in the rural areas, which lack a thrust in terms of regional and national development. Besides the long-term dangers inherent in the bypassing of government, NGOs have also been blamed for poor knowledge transfer. Many local ones lack the resources to do a good job of the intermediation of resources and ideas.

Uganda is still a very poor country, with some of the lowest social achievement indicators in Africa. Aid will thus continue to be a key source of development resources for a number of years to come. It is thus necessary to improve the government's capacity to absorb aid and to see to it that undue appreciation of the shilling due to inflows of donor assistance is prevented. Since an appreciation hurts exports, it is the equivalent of a tax on the countryside in favour of consumers of imported goods, usually urban based. In order for the country to eventually escape dependence on aid, it is necessary to put in place measures to attract other forms of long-term capital. Development of the private sector will be crucial in this regard.

I.9. Issues arising: Security, East African cooperation and politics

Domestic insecurity and crisis in the Great Lakes

The Ugandan economy is much stronger today than during the civil war of the early 1980s. Still, there is concern that the increased regional insecurity might disrupt the government's focus on political and economic reform and that in the military theatres human rights abuses of the past might return. For more than a decade, the Uganda government has been fighting the Lord's Resistance Army (LRA) in northern Uganda, which started as a band of soldiers fleeing Museveni's advance in the 1980s but has since become a real obstacle to peace and development in the northern part of the country. Subsequently, Museveni has tried to lure the northern population by introducing a Northern Uganda Reconstruction Programme, supported by a number of donors including the World Bank, and appointing a Resident Minister for the North.

Still, the insurgence has continued to affect all aspects of life in Gulu and Kitgum as well as surrounding districts. Rebels have attacked schools and hospitals, while students and medical workers have been abducted and the battles have ruined the infrastructure and peasant farms. The Uganda Parliament set up a committee to investigate the northern insurrection, which summoned many politicians, businessmen and lay people from the North as well as other areas of the country. Some testimonies before the committee were fairly predictable, including the charge that politicians from the North have been sidelined within Museveni's NRM. The national army has also been accused of harassing the local population in the course of their anti-guerrilla operations. In May 1999, during a tour of the North, Museveni announced a "blanket amnesty" for the leader of the LRA and his rebels, if they surrendered their arms and returned to their communities.

Of even more serious political and economic consequence has been Uganda's military involvement in the Democratic Republic of the Congo, with which it shares an 800 kilometre long border. The government has argued that its military presence there is solely for purposes of national security, notably to ensure that opponents of the government did not launch attacks on Uganda from the Congo. Until recently, this line of reasoning found some sympathy among the population and the donors. However, there is no doubt that a continued military presence in the Congo has already had a distracting effect on policy. It draws real resources away from the social sectors and also creates tension domestically and in the region. The conflict has also taken regional dimensions, involving up to seven African countries. In economic terms disruptions at the borders have become very costly. First, they lower the degree of economic integration, leading to losses of markets, not only for the most vulnerable members in society, the peasant farmers, but also for regular trade between countries. As a result of these low intensity civil wars, there has also been a serious increase in the flow of arms to the region, raising the level of insecurity. However, as in other parts of the world, disengagement from military conflict can be a tough and prolonged process. Moreover, critics of the government have argued that since the rebel groups in Western Uganda have continued to murder and harass civilians, in spite of the military intervention in the Congo, the *cordon sanitaire* that the presence of Ugandan troops was supposed to create has not been effective. Uganda has a fairly high political risk rating and its involvement in the Congo has increased it further.

East African co-operation

East African economic co-operation is finally taking concrete shape. Policy-makers have taken a slower and more careful path to renewed co-operation, probably mindful of the disruptive impact of the earlier breakdown of the community close to 20 years ago. A major emphasis has been on involving as many stakeholders as possible. In Uganda, therefore, meetings have taken place to sensitise the various groups and to bring on board their suggestions and concerns. In introducing the first East African passport, which allows holders to travel unhindered within the region, policymakers have likewise had their eye on public opinion. The regional secretariat at Arusha has been expanded and is assuming a higher profile in the co-ordination of regional issues, recently adding a military liaison office (see also Kayizzi-Mugerwa, 1997).

The Ministers of Finance now read their budget speeches on the same day in July, although there is still little direct policy co-ordination. There is also increasing co-operation in the area of crime fighting, with the Attorneys-General of the three countries meeting regularly. In the financial area, the chairmen of the stock exchanges have also met, with the Kenyan stock ex-change providing assistance to the newer and smaller bourses in Uganda and Tanzania. An important new regional project concerns improving the envi-ronment in and around Lake Victoria. Though the lake is a major source of food and water, and provides transport routes, it has been poorly taken care of in the past decades, leading to the accumulation of effluents.

However, East Africa's older concerns will take much longer to go away. A cause of serious friction in the earlier co-operation was the feeling that Kenyan companies were taking advantage of Uganda and Tanzania's indus-trial backwardness to capture market share. This then prevented them from industrial development. Although the poorer countries have established some industries during the era of adjustment, which could compete reasonably well with those in Kenya, the latter is still the undisputed economic leader in the region and businessmen from Kenya have invested heavily in Uganda. On the other hand, Uganda has a comparative advantage in food production, notably maize. However, Kenyan food markets are far from open. Another area of potential friction is taxation policy harmonisation. The huge discrepancies between Kenyan taxes and those of Uganda, and to a lesser extent Tanzania, have led to the smuggling of goods across the borders and Lake Victoria. This has been most notable with respect to fuel. Since Uganda's fuel taxes are much higher than those of its neighbours there has been much fuel smuggling with serious effects on government revenue. The proposed removal of tariffs in the East African region by the year 2000 is thus contentious, and already there is speculation that the proposed signing of the Treaty in mid-1999 might be "piecemeal" with the difficult issues left pending.

Thus while there is much benefit in closer East African cooperation, in-deed Rwanda and Burundi have already applied for entry, the realities on the ground would seem to suggest a much slower pace than currently envisaged.

However, a slow but steady pace need not be a bad thing. The earlier break-up was partly because many crucial factors had been glossed over in the haste to arrive at political and economic unity.

Political developments

After 13 years in power, many have begun to note signs of fatigue among the ranks of the National Resistance Movement. However, at its National Executive Committee meeting held in April 1999, the leaders were in combative mood. They seem bent, as sanctioned by the Constitution, on pushing through a referendum in 2000 to determine whether the country should continue to be governed by the "movement", that is a one-party political system or whether to allow a multiparty system of politics. Pundits have little doubt that the NRM will be able to command a majority for a continuation of the "movement" system. This is partly because multiparty advocates have had very little opportunity to canvas for pluralism. Still, a long incumbency has its own peculiar problems. The population might cease to see the problems confronting the country as those of underdevelopment and instead associate their persistence to the leader and the system. It is thus to Museveni's credit that his political capital, though somewhat diminished, is still sufficient to see him through another gruelling decade at the helm. But as he readily admits Uganda is not his private property and he will some day have to move on.

I.10. Concluding remarks

In Part I, we have tried to highlight policies and performance in Uganda since the 1960s, with emphasis on the period since 1987 when Museveni's government embarked on wide-ranging economic reforms. Experience shows that few African countries have been able to maintain high average growth rates for any appreciable period. While a number like Côte d'Ivoire did well for limited periods, they fell into serious recession in the 1970s and 80s. The issue here is whether Uganda will be able to sustain the high growth rates that it has seen since 1987. Some of this growth obviously is a catching-up of the lost years between 1971 and 1986. There is little doubt, however, that much of it has been made possible by the adoption of sensible policies, not least the stabilisation of the economy and removal of controls on economic activities.

However, a number of issues remain. Uganda's social indicators are poorer than those of countries at the same level of average income. Its education status lags behind that of its neighbours, morbidity and mortality levels are high, while much of the infrastructure is still poorly developed. Governance and the rule of law have been emphasised in the past decade, but there remains a lot to be done in strengthening the police and the judiciary. However, the above are not issues that the government is unwilling to implement. For a reforming government that does not want to regress into controls and declining growth, they cannot be avoided. To maintain credibility in its policies, mobilise domestic support as well as that of the donors, the main ingredients of the government's reform programme will have to remain in place.

STATISTICAL ANNEX

Table A1. *Rate of growth of real GDP at factor cost by sector (%) (1991 prices)*

	Monetary Agriculture	Mining	Manuf.	El & Water	Con-struction	Trade	Hotels & Rest	Trpt &Com	Ser-vices	Non-Monetary	TOTAL
1988	6.8	-5.5	16.1	6.4	4.9	11.5	8.4	5.5	6.3	5.6	7.1
1989	5.8	15.3	11.6	2.2	6.6	7.3	13	5.2	7	5.4	6.4
1990	7.4	165.6	5.3	1.6	5.8	6.9	11.6	7.6	8.6	1.6	5.5
1991	5.1	31.1	11.9	11.4	6.4	7.3	17.5	7.8	8.8	0.4	5.2
1992	5	7.9	7.9	9.1	5	3.9	12	4.4	8.8	1.1	4.5
1993	6.6	11.8	12.5	1.7	11	6.3	16.3	8.4	6.7	3.2	6.3
1994	8.4	-4.8	17.9	13.2	23.5	15.6	24.8	14.1	6.9	4.7	10.1
1995	8	28.2	18.3	9.9	19.2	16.3	11.8	13.5	6.5	2	8.4
1996	3.9	47.7	14.7	11.8	17.2	4.1	7.2	9.6	6	-1.2	5.1
1997	0.6	48.7	15.3	8.2	14.1	3.7	5.6	17.1	8.4	0.4	5.2

Source: Ministry of Finance and Economic Development, Statistical Abstract 1998, p. 32.

Table A2. *Sectoral share of GDP at factor cost (1991 prices)*

	Monetary Agriculture	Mining	Manuf.	El & Water	Con-struction	Trade	Hotels & Rest	Trpt &Com	Ser-vices	Non-Monetary	TOTAL
1988	24.2	0.1	5.3	0.9	5	10.9	1	4.1	14.2	34.4	100
1989	24	0.1	5.5	0.8	5	11	1.1	4	14.3	34.1	100
1990	24.5	0.2	5.5	0.8	5	11.1	1.1	4.1	14.7	32.8	100
1991	24.5	0.3	5.9	0.8	5.1	11.4	1.3	4.2	15.2	31.4	100
1992	24.6	0.3	6.1	0.9	5.1	11.3	1.4	4.2	15.8	30.3	100
1993	24.7	0.3	6.4	0.8	5.3	11.3	1.5	4.3	15.9	29.4	100
1994	24.3	0.3	6.9	0.9	6	12.2	1.7	4.4	15.4	28	100
1995	23.7	0.3	7.5	0.9	6.6	13.1	1.8	4.7	15.2	26.3	100
1996	23.5	0.5	8.2	0.9	7.3	12.9	1.8	4.9	15.3	24.8	100
1997	22.4	0.7	9	1	8	12.7	1.8	5.4	15.5	23.6	100

Source: Ministry of Finance and Economic Development, Statistical Abstract 1988, p. 36.

UGANDA INVESTMENT AUTHORITY

Since its foundation in 1991, the UIA has licensed 2,417 domestic and foreign firms undertaking investment in Uganda. The Authority was conceived as a one-stop shop where investors could process all requirements and licences. First, it would issue an investment licence, on presentation of a business plan, and subsequently a certificate of incentives to qualified investors. Other services included assisting investors to clear capital goods imports through customs, obtaining industrial land for establishing production facilities, utilities and related services. Of the total number of projects licensed since 1991, over 96 per cent were duly established.

Table B.1 presents data on accumulated planned investment in Uganda collected by the Uganda Investment Authority (UIA). The figures for planned investment are available because they are those presented to the UIA at project inception. However, it is rather difficult to determine with certainty how much of this investment actually takes place (see below), but the figures are useful as proxies of investor intentions.

Table B.1. *Uganda Investment Authority: Licensed projects by sector (1991–1998, US$, %)*

Sector	Projects Licensed	Planned Investment US$	Planned Employment	Planned investment per Job (US$)
Agriculture, forestry & fishing	614	875,036,427	60,444	14,487
Construction	124	187,486,888	10,283	18,203
Financial services	10	7,140,000	324	22,037
Insurance and business services	219	317,639,471	12,903	24,617
Manufacturing	648	2,007,766,547	38,797	51,751
Mining and quarrying	40	235,296,960	6,480	36,311
Personal and social services	64	56,903,715	3,283	17,333
Property development	119	500,891,550	6,335	79,067
Tourism	202	389,406,414	12,088	32,214
Trade and restaurants	202	107,997,659	5,502	19,629
Transport, communications and storage	175	417,460,886	9,232	45,219
Total	2,417	5,103,026,517	165,671	30,802
Memoranda items:				
Joint venture	616	1,843,855,063	48,119	38,414
Foreign	898	1,678,450,602	54,069	31,082
Local	813	1,300,112,511	55,510	23,426

Source: Uganda Investment Authority (1998).

One of the main goals of the investment promotion undertaken by the UIA is the creation of employment. We have tried to estimate the average investment needed to create a job in the various sectors. The biggest number of projects were in manufacturing, followed closely by agriculture, forestry and fishing. However, the latter sectors have the largest planned employment and thus the lowest investment per job created, lower than US$ 15,000. This is followed by personal and social services at about US$ 17,300 per job and construction at an investment of US$ 18,200 per job. Notably, the investment cost of a job in manufacturing is over US$ 50,000. This is three times as much as in agriculture, forestry and fishing. This figure is high, both in comparison to other sectors, and with respect to neighbouring countries. A recent study of Kenyan manufacturing found the average establishment costs per worker to be only half as much (Bigsten et al., 1998). Such a high initial investment outlay per worker implies that the technologies used are fairly advanced, but could also reflect on the still fairly poor manning capacities in Uganda, with technical skills too confined to meet the demands of a rapidly expanding sector. In a UIA survey on problems faced by the new investors, a larger proportion of foreign and joint venture investors found lack of trained manpower to be a serious problem. Lack of basic utilities, or their unreliability, forces investors to install own aggregates. Investors thus take recourse to capital intensive techniques.

When investments are split by investor type, an interesting trend emerges. Foreign financed projects have exceeded those by local people, while a number of joint ventures have been undertaken as well. However, there is a wide difference in investment outlay per worker between joint ventures (US$ 38,400), and foreign and local investors (US$ 31,000 compared to less than US$ 23,500). Thus while the average investment per project differs only slightly, local investors seem to create more jobs for less investment. In fact local projects dominate in sectors with the lowest planned investment per job created, such as agriculture, social services and construction. They are thus more likely, in the short-run to have a higher impact on the huge unemployment and underemployment in the country. In the longer term, however, the results will depend on the overall dynamics generated in the economy. That is, on the rate of growth of the established firms, their exit as well as the entry of new ones.

Part II
Macroeconomic policies to promote stability

II.1. Public finance

II.1.1. Introduction

Public finances have been at the centre of Uganda's reform effort in the past decade. The goal has been fourfold: to maintain macroeconomic stability, increase the efficiency of public expenditure, devise less distortionary and equitable methods of taxation, and develop managerial and institutional capacities in both taxation and expenditure. A fifth goal, voiced frequently in budget speeches, has been to reduce Uganda's aid dependence. However, although the government has been able to increase its revenue collection in the past few years, public resources remain low and vulnerable. The public sector's capacity to address poverty via its own resources is all but impossible. Donor aid thus continues to be a key resource input in the economy. This implies in turn that a number of crucial initiatives, such as the anti-poverty measures, will remain donor driven (Goetz and Jenkins, 1998), with threats to local ownership and sustainability.

However, in spite of progress, it has been difficult for the government to achieve the goals that it has set for itself in the fiscal area. The recent literature on the dynamics of transition from war to peace (Collier and Gunning, 1995; Bevan, 1994) suggests that while the fiscal implications of a return to peace often are benign, the new situation also implies shifts in private portfolios that might have perverse effects. It is also obvious that a government at the head of a conquering guerrilla army has initially a difficult job of fence-mending and domestic reconciliation, both of which have implications for domestic expenditure. Thus the restructuring of the civil service and privatisation, both with substantial fiscal implications, were not to be embarked on until the government had secured itself in Kampala.

II.1.2. Revenue

In comparison to many countries in Africa, even those that have experienced a prolonged period of political destabilisation and civil war, the government's capacity to generate revenue has been below average. This is partly a result of the earlier crisis, which saw the government losing credibility with coffee farmers, who contributed both directly and indirectly to government revenue, and partly to the small size of the formal sector, notably the private sector. The latter had suffered a major shock when Amin expelled Asian business owners from Uganda. In the absence of audited records, those who had taken over from the Asians were taxed by means of "tax deposits". The intention had been to undertake the final tax assessment afterwards. Although this raised the amount of collusion in the system, a return to normal taxation was not possible until the mid-1990s.

Table II.1 presents figures on Uganda's revenue (excluding grants) from fiscal 1991/92. As a percentage of GDP, revenue at 11.5 per cent of GDP in 1997/98 though a remarkable improvement from 7 per cent of GDP in 1991/92, means that revenue effort is still much lower than the African average, which is well above 20 per cent (African Development Bank, 1998). For example Tanzania's was close to 17 per cent while that for Kenya was double Uganda's. However, while Uganda was realising a close to 1 per cent increase in revenue as a percentage of GDP since the early 1990s, this flattened out in 1996/97 even declining slightly in fiscal 1997/98. This has been blamed on falling administrative efficiency and failure to expand the tax net.

Table II.1 *Sources of government revenue 1991/92–1996/97 (bn shs and %)*

	1991/92	1992/93	1993/94	1994/95	1995/96	1996/97	1997/98
Revenue % of GDP	184.1	288.5	399.2	537.2	647.6	776.3	810.5
Revenue Sources %	7	8	9.8	10.8	11.5	11.8	11.5
Income tax	12.8	14	14.4	14.5	12.8	13	14.5
Indirect taxes	85.2	85.2	83.9	83.8	86	86	81
Other revenue	2.0	0.8	1.7	1.7	1.2	1.0	4.5

Source: Republic of Uganda, Ministry of Planning and Economic Development; Background to the Budget (various issues).

Trade taxes have traditionally been a major source of government revenue in Uganda, a situation not very different from that of its neighbours. But here, they became even more entrenched since the chaos of the past decades had ruined the records of income tax authorities. Tariffs have contributed about 35 per cent of recurrent revenue in the 1990s. However, export taxes per se have not been a large item. Abolished earlier in response to the persuasive arguments of not taxing poor farmers, they were briefly introduced during the coffee boom (1994–96) although even then yielding very little revenue.

Among customs duties, energy taxes (especially petrol) have been the biggest source of government revenue. Although petrol taxes are common in Africa because of easy collection, they are particularly high in Uganda. As we noted above, this has led to smuggling of fuel products from neighbouring countries. However, since Uganda is a land-locked country with high transport costs, the petrol tax has a high incidence on exporters as well as on the remoter regions of the country such as Northern Uganda. There is thus need for a structural shift in the tax base away from taxes on petrol towards income tax (today lightly taxed by Sub-Saharan African comparison). In the 1997 Budget, duty on petrol was reduced from 225 to 215 per cent, diesel from 170 to 160 per cent, and paraffin from 115 to 105 per cent.

Improvements in revenues over the past decade have been the result of a more organised tax collection effort, spearheaded by the Uganda Revenue Authority. The government introduced a 17 per cent VAT in July 1996 to replace sales tax and the commercial transactions levy (CTL) first introduced in 1972. The objective was to broaden the tax base and to increase revenue collected. It is hoped that the uniform tax rate will reduce the need for detailed information and thus the cost of administration. It could also help reduce tax evasion. Another advantage is that a VAT avoids the distortions associated with the taxation of factors of production such as labour. A drawback may be, however, that due to its uniformity, the distributional implications of the VAT may be negative. Many industrialists found VAT of 17 per cent too high, especially when compared to Kenya's 15 per cent (and in light of the latter's lower production costs and easier access to the sea). In 1996/97 VAT accounted for 43 per cent of revenue (excluding grants). However, while overall revenues increased, the VAT contribution in 1997/98 fell to about 31 per cent. This was blamed euphemistically on "lack of administrative efficiency" at the URA, a reference to high levels of corruption in the URA and the failure of the Ministry of Finance to sanction poor performance.

Direct taxes still comprise only a modest percentage of total revenue. Income taxes have not contributed more than 15 per cent of domestic revenue in the 1990s (Table II.1). In a bid to boost the revenue effort, a number of innovations have been introduced in the past few years. From fiscal 1996/97 the government started paying taxes on its own purchases. This was meant to limit the corruption that characterised government purchases in the past, with private importers bringing in goods duty free by claiming that they belonged to the government. The government has also embarked on tax education, to expand the tax base and increase tax compliance. The goal is to improve the tax culture by pointing at some of the benefits of a higher tax effort, notably the financing of universal primary education. It has also been argued that increased accountability in public life will help boost the confidence of the taxpayer.

The government also needs to find ways of widening its tax base to include more groups than is currently the case. Many of Uganda's self-employed and agricultural producers are not paying income taxes. Furthermore, fishermen on the islands of Lake Victoria as well as Uganda's other lakes are largely outside the tax net. In the past, it was difficult to justify a rapid extension of the tax net when social services to most of the country remained so poor. However, the universal primary education programme noted above, provides the government with some arguments for a broader tax effort.[4]

Key policy concerns are now the long-term viability of the government's revenues as well as soundness of its expenditure. Both are crucial for the success of the government's poverty reduction strategy and, generally, for sustaining growth. By the mid-1990s, the government had increased current

---

4. Matovu (1998a, b) undertakes an analysis of the welfare impact of the tax reform in Uganda using micro data. He concludes that the distributional impact is small, although the households in the lowest deciles lose. This is related to the implications of the tax structure on income and expenditure streams of the poorest households.

revenues to such a level that they covered current expenditures (which have also expanded in real terms). However, this has to some extent been achieved at the cost of distorting resource allocation in the economy. The incentive structure for private investors as well as other economic actors has been negatively affected, while lack of a long-term tax strategy, notably with regard to investment incentives and a functioning duty draw back mechanism, has led to destabilising swings in policy. As noted above, recent policies are aimed at remedying these shortcomings. In December 1997, a new Income Tax Law was introduced, with the goal of extending the tax base, notably a presumptive tax was introduced for the informal sector, and reducing tax rates in the medium term. A Tax Tribunal is now in place to adjudicate cases related to taxation, which have often held up private sector operations.

II.1.3 Expenditure

Besides policy commitment, Uganda's much lauded reform has been a result of rapidly rising expenditure. In the past decade, the size of domestic revenues has not been a serious constraint on government expenditure thanks to foreign aid. For example while recurrent revenue was 7 per cent of GDP in 1991/92, recurrent expenditure was close to 11 per cent higher. It was not until the mid-1990s that government was able to cover its recurrent expenditures with its own money. But owing to the fungibility of money, aid still plays a role in recurrent expenditure.

Still, while tax revenues have increased, the budgetary process remains weak. Dependence on cash budgets since 1992 has meant that the Finance Minister has had to undertake supplementary allocations in the course of the fiscal year. However, in the competition for resources between, say, health and education and defence, the latter often gets the resources it needs while projects in the social sectors are scaled down for lack of funds. Given this underlying inequality of distribution, it is doubtful whether increased revenue on its own can resolve the problem of fiscal efficacy. Though the goal of the cash budget was to eliminate payment arrears, which had distorted macroeconomic policy in the past, promissory notes have been issued by ministries in recent years in anticipation of supplementary allocations which sometimes did not materialise. Administrative inefficiency in the banking system, notably the poor performance of the Uganda Commercial Bank which does most of the government's transactions, has also affected the flow of funds making payments difficult.

Table II.2 shows that in the early 1990s, the government made some attempts to shift expenditure in favour of the social sectors. However, increasing military pressures have forced the government to swing back. Thus while defence expenditure had fallen to 15 per cent of total outlays by fiscal 1992/93 when the troubles in Northern Uganda had subsided, it rose quickly once again and was up to 20 per cent in 1994/95. However, since the military also had a high call on resources in other areas of expenditure, such as public order, its overall claim on the budget was quite high. Still, it is puzzling that although the military excursion into the Congo would have implied increases in total expenditures from fiscal 1996/97 onwards, official figures (Table II.2) indicate otherwise. There is speculation that some of the money funding the war could be from the privatisation receipts, especially since the privatisation account is now officially "empty". However, the government can also raise war expenditure via reallocation within the defence budget. For example, increases in current military expenditure were possible in fiscal 1998/99 thanks to the shifting of funds from the "clearance of arrears and promissory notes" vote to current expenditure. However, many now blame the economic setbacks of the first half of 1999, especially the depreciation of the shilling, on Uganda's military involvement in the Congo.[5]

Museveni has argued, however, that without security all other attempts at economic development would be futile. Indeed during the CG meetings held in Kampala in 1998, he referred to the army as the "burglar proofing" of the economy. In any case as long as the regional insecurity persists, the government will be very unwilling to reduce its defence expenditure by much. However, the military could also be exposed to some of the restructuring and efficiency measures currently done in the rest of the public sector. This will help lower costs, reduce corruption in military purchases and increase general accountability. Since the army is an important institution, its improved efficiency is bound to impact positively on the rest of the economy.

Table II.2 shows that the last years have seen a radical shift in expenditures on education. The recent introduction of universal primary education (UPE) doubled the intake of children of primary school age. It proved to be a popular reform and is credited for Museveni's re-election in 1996. However, to be effective the UPE reform will demand even more expenditure outlays both recurrent and capital as schools are built and teachers trained. In contrast, health expenditures remain very low, only about 5 per cent. Within the sector, the old expenditure discrepancies (the bulk of expenditure is on Mulago, the university hospital) persist.

Loan repayments have been a big budget item. In the early 1990s, they accounted for over a third of recurrent expenditure. However, a combination of debt forgiveness and debt rescheduling including the newly implemented HIPC programme have lowered the debt burden.

Uganda's development expenditure budget is almost entirely financed by donor money. Table II.3 presents the development expenditure shares. As observed earlier, donor funding has enabled the country to undertake expenditure that would have taken it a long time to reach on its own. It has also helped instil a sense of efficiency in resource use during a period of severe shortage of finances. Even here, the education sector has seen a rapid increase

---

5. In March 1999, the IMF, for the first time in 7 years, temporarily suspended the release of a tranche of an ESAF loan to Uganda, to show its displeasure with the expenditure numbers, which had overshot target. However, Bank of Uganda officials indicate that the margins involved were fairly small and could have been ignored in the past but that the IMF wanted to assert its position and that of the donors who want more social and not military expenditure.

in expenditure outlays, essentially on the construction of classrooms and purchase of equipment. However, some of the development expenditure under "economic services" actually refers to expenditure undertaken within the Ministry of Finance and Economic Planning, such as purchase of computers and cars for project supervision, and might not be development expenditure in the conventional meaning.

Table II.2. *Functional analysis of recurrent expenditure 1991/92–1997/98 (%)*

	1991/92	1992/93	1993/94	1994/95	1995/96	1996/97	1997/98
General public administration	16.9	28.7	26.7	30.5	23.7	20.6	20.5
Defence	18.7	15.1	17.2	20.1	20.3	19.5	15.4
Public order	5.9	4.5	6.4	8.7	8.9	8.9	7.5
Education	15.5	11.9	10.3	11	19	23.6	21.7
Health	4.5	4.1	4	3.9	5.6	5.4	4.9
Community & social services	1.3	1.2	1.7	1.2	1.2	1.2	0.9
Economic services	6	4.4	6.1	5.8	3.2	3.4	3.5
Interest on public debt	na	na	na	na	na	0.3	8.1
Loan repayment	31.1	30.2	27.7	18.7	16.6	16.4	16.5
Other	0.1	na	na	na	1.2	0.8	0.8

Source: Republic of Uganda, Ministry of Planning and Economic Development; Background to the Budget (various issues).

Table II.3. *Functional analysis of development expenditure 1991/92–1997/98 (%)*

	1991/92	1992/93	1993/94	1994/95	1995/96	1996/97
General public administration	37.1	47.4	38	43.4	23	15.1
Defence	11	3.3	8.6	5.2	8.2	4.3
Public order	4.5	4.5	10.1	4.7	5.3	3.1
Education	3.8	9.8	11.2	9.4	7.8	9.9
Health	8.7	8.5	10.1	5.9	7.1	11.6
Community & social services	0.4	2.3	7.2	1	0.9	2.1
Economic services	34.4	24.2	14.9	24.5	41.9	51.7
Entandikwa credit scheme	-	-	-	5.8	3.9	2.1

Source: Republic of Uganda, Ministry of Planning and Economic Development; Background to the Budget (various issues).

In the medium term, the demands on the central budget are bound to increase: adding to UPE, the emphasis on primary health care services is also going to be resource intensive. All these demands imply that expenditure will have to rise rather than fall. To prevent non-sustainable deficits, however, new source of revenue will have to be found, or current expenditures, such as those on subsidies to parastatals will have to be curtailed. An added challenge will be to define tax structures that are close to those of Uganda's regional trading partners (in many cases this will necessitate tax reductions) in order to reduce the smuggling of goods that is rampant and enable policy convergence.

Alongside the macroeconomic reforms, Uganda has also embarked on an ambitious decentralisation programme. There is concern that given the weak management structures at the central level, the funds allotted by the government to the district level, where structures are even weaker, might lead to leakage. In attempts to devise ways to improve the delivery of resources from the centre to the periphery, a tracking mechanism was developed and tested with World Bank supervision. It was found that although some resources reached the district level, much could be done to reduce waste at that level.

In budgeting, the government aspires to an outcomes-oriented process, where clearly defined objectives determine resource flows. In this context, the supplementary expenditures used by the government to cover budgetary "holes", even though remaining within the strictures of the cash budget framework, have a disorienting impact on the prioritisation framework towards which the government is striving. In the 1997 Budget Speech, supplementary budgets were suspended. Furthermore, strict budgetary management and monitoring was introduced to ensure that there is no diversion of funds from sub-sectors. It has also become necessary to restructure the budgeting process in order to reflect the changed sector priorities. Notably, the focus on poverty eradication.

II.2. Exchange rate policy

The history of exchange rate reforms in Uganda is closely related to the economic management abilities of the various regimes. The exchange rate reform attempts under Obote were initially quite successful, but met with resistance as the economy deteriorated. The initial exchange rate policy under the NRM was unrealistic and counterproductive, based on controls. This was soon reversed and the policies adopted in 1987 eventually led to a market-determined exchange rate. In 1988, the government introduced further reforms, with the shilling devalued by 60 per cent to 150 shillings to the dollar, reducing the parallel market premium, but failing to eliminate it completely. In 1990 foreign exchange bureaux were introduced, thus legalizing the black market. They bought and sold foreign exchange with no questions asked. The parallel market premium which was several hundred per cent in 1986 and 1987 came down gradually and by 1993 it had been eliminated.[6] An Inter-Bank Foreign Exchange Market was put in place the 1st of November 1993 to support efforts to attain market-based exchange rate management. This was introduced alongside the elimination of restrictions on all international current account transactions. Then the capital account was fully liberalized in July 1997 (Kasekende, Kitabire and Martin, 1998).

For much of the adjustment period the Bank of Uganda did not have an exchange-rate target. Its main concern was to smooth out exchange-rate fluctuations. One might say that a balanced budget was perhaps the nominal anchor, but with increasing revenues (largely from aid) leading to a fiscal surplus this approach was no longer viable. The government was then left

---

6. The black market premium was 306% in 1986, 200% in 1987, 118% in 1988, 67% in 1989, 27% in 1990, 21 % in 1991, and 8% in 1992. Thereafter it was essentially eliminated, Ssemogerere and Kalema (1998, p. 21).

with two choices for nominal anchor: the exchange rate or the money supply. The volatility of the money supply during the subsequent period meant that it was not an appropriate anchor, leaving the exchange rate as the natural choice.

Higher coffee prices and an essentially market determined foreign exchange rate after the abolition of the auction in 1993 led to huge inflows of foreign currency. This tended to appreciate the shilling with an unfavourable impact on the profitability of exports, notably coffee sales. A strong shilling also had a negative impact on the government budget, since the amount of shillings realised from balance-of-payments support funds fell. Still, in the new liberalised economic environment, the system led to higher imports, which helped limit the effect of the inflow and contain inflation. The Bank of Uganda intervened to some extent on the foreign-exchange market to ensure that the shilling did not appreciate too much.

During the following years the country saw a combination of increasing money supply, falling inflation, and steady exchange rate, which seems puzzling. Between 1994 and 1996, for example, broad money increased by about 25 per cent annually, while inflation was below 10 per cent (Mbire, 1997a). This indicates that there was a process of financial deepening. Henstridge (1995) suggests that from an initially very low level of monetisation, large percentage increases in money supply may be non-inflationary if there is a combination of increases in the transactions and asset demand for money. This seems to be the case in Uganda.

Managing the increased coffee-export inflow in 1994–95 was a test of economic management in the new liberalised environment. The money had a real potential for destabilising the economy by appreciating the currency. The government decided to introduce a coffee tax as the quickest means of mopping up extra liquidity in the market. This tax was not introduced until January 1995, as there seemed to be little currency appreciation, or even inflation. It was already reduced in the budget for 1995/96 and abolished completely the following year. Generally, the system managed to absorb the windfall in a reasonably efficient way.

In the past couple of years, coffee prices have weakened and there has been a gradual depreciation of the shilling. The Bank of Uganda does not have a target for the exchange rate, however, although it intervenes at times to reduce the fluctuations in the exchange rate. Generally, the exchange rate reflects the level of Uganda's competitiveness, although one may still be concerned about the appreciation caused by the substantial aid inflow. It may lock Uganda in a state of aid dependence with unfortunate consequences for long-term competitiveness and growth. Recent studies at the OECD Development Centre on a number of African countries (see Sekkat and Varoudakis, 1998; Richaud and Varoudakis, 1999) have estimated the degree to which the real exchange rate in Uganda has been overvalued over the period 1970–91 (see Table II.4). The Table suggests that the overvaluation was most serious in the mid-1970s and the early 1990s. There has then been a gradual convergence towards zero, although the economy was still not there in 1996. The over-valuation is blamed on excessively inward oriented policies, and its reduction on increased openness.

Table 11.4. *Exchange rate misalignment 1970–1996*

Year	Real exchange rate misalignment	Real exchange ratemisalignment (excluding terms of trade effect)
1970	0,227091	0,211944
1971	0,207006	0,206112
1972	0,370766	0,334264
1973	0,530782	0,476935
1974	0,604753	0,469979
1975	0,778740	0,666064
1976	0,555345	0,664023
1977	0,297448	0,724301
1978	0,265128	0,433590
1979	0,081487	0,229296
1980	-9,24850E	0,132198
1981	0,115137	0,148892
1982	-0,122879	-0,090044
1983	0,132602	0,203150
1984	0,115627	0,298181
1985	0,161525	0,353582
1986	0,014497	0,255317
1987	0,136388	0,161217
1988	0,072021	0,143465
1989	0,203678	0,174463
1990	0,322339	0,188326
1991	0,332911	0,206143
1992	0,493482	0,220352
1993	0,392613	0,228703
1994	0,261264	0,219274
1995	-0,002501	0,113164
1996	-3,00227E	0,067170

Source: Sekkat and Varoudakis (1997).

II.3. The debt burden

II.3.1. Introduction

In the introductory chapter, we spelled out the criteria for an emerging economy with the level of external indebtedness being one of them. Debt levels do matter for three reasons: 1) The stock of outstanding debt deters investments because of the threats of the debt overhang. 2) The stock of debt and constant rescheduling sharpen the sense of dependence on outsiders. 3) The large gross flows giving smaller net flows, distort decision making and take up valuable time.

Though crucial to Uganda's economic rehabilitation, foreign assistance led to a high level of indebtedness. With regard to debt sustainability, the main concern relates to the appropriate use of the available resources. Uganda has gone beyond the stage of emergency repairs, even that of rehabilitation, and needs to plan its aid resources better in order to ensure high growth. Poor planning has in the past led to problems of aid absorption. Generally, inadequate institutional capacities, especially in the line ministries and at the Bank of Uganda, were blamed for the slow pace of project implementation and the speedy utilisation of disbursed funds. In responding to these micro deficiencies, some donors, such as Sweden, used their aid budgets to pay off Uganda's debt arrears, especially to the World Bank, under a scheme referred to as the Fifth Dimension. By resolving the arrears problem with the IBRD loans (that is the harder loans of the World Bank proper) Uganda has then had access to the much softer loans from the IDA.

II.3.2. Policy on debt

Uganda's debt policy was more or less dictated from abroad. Initially the new NRM government had hoped to get funding from where it could, sometimes including loans acquired on more or less commercial terms. However, when the adjustment programmes were embarked on it was agreed that the government would not borrow from sources other than those which ensured a high grant element. Since regular debt servicing ensured a continuous flow of resources, the government chose to pay off debts and to clear arrears so as to remain on good terms with the important creditors. The debt strategy was roughly as follows: multilateral debt and Paris Club debt had to be repaid, whenever possible; positive net flows had to be ensured, either via rescheduling, forgiveness or new loans; limits had to be imposed on non-concessionary borrowing (or as we noted above a total stop to such borrowing); short-term repayment arrangements on all the country's loans had to be eliminated. The strategy towards bilateral lenders was mixed, however. For important trade partners such as India, China, and even North Korea, which had agreed to undertake rescheduling, their debts were duly serviced. However, for others, such as Tanzania, Burundi, and Russia, which had not reached formal agreements with the government, the whole debt situation was ignored.[7] However, during the course of Uganda's efforts to reach "completion point" that is to satisfy the terms of the HIPC initiative, the country made efforts to reach settlement on the remaining arrears to the Abu Dhabi Fund, China, India, Iraq, Libya, Pakistan, Burundi, Democratic People's Republic of Korea, Nigeria, and some commercial creditors.

In spite of a policy aimed at getting maximum debt relief from the Paris Club, write-off or long-term rescheduling of non-OECD debt, commercial debt buyback and strict limitations on new borrowing, except on the most concessional terms, Table II.5 shows that total debt continued to expand in the 1990s. However, this was perhaps not as fast as in the second half of the 1980s,

---

7. The debts owed to these three countries are rather unconventional. Tanzanian debts were incurred during the war against Amin, when the bulk of the fighting force was composed of Tanzanians. Burundi supplied emergency services and goods to the NRM in its first year in power. Russian debts are related to arms supplies, including those to Amin.

when large amounts of multilateral funds were received by the government for rehabilitation purposes.

Though there exist a whole range of indicators of external viability, a recent ESAF evaluation (Botchwey et al., 1998) chose as the numerator either debt service (flow variable), debt outstanding or net present value. For the denominator they use either exports or GDP. They argue, however, that too much weight has been given to the ratios that relate debt service to exports, and that the most relevant comparison is vis-à-vis GDP. On the basis of these indicators the situation of Uganda has improved considerably between 1992 and 1996, mainly because rapid growth has increased the debt carrying capacity of the country. The foreign debt is still sizeable, though (see Tables II.5–6).

Table II.5. Uganda debt statistics, 1990–96 (US$ million, %)

	1990	1991	1992	1993	1994	1995	1996
Total debt stock ($)	2583	2777	2928	3029	3372	3573	3674
Debt/Exports (%)	1050	1375	1471	1252	980	523	492
Debt/GNP (%)	61.1	85.1	105.6	95.5	85.6	62.8	60.5
Debt service/Exports (%)	59.9	73.3	57.3	64.7	43.7	20	20
Multilateral/Total debt (%)	49.2	51.3	53.3	57	59.7	61.8	62.2
Rescheduling ($)	18	9	100	38	0	17.2	-
Debt reduction ($)	50	1	14	138	7	42	0

Source: OECD data files.

Table II.6. *Uganda: Net present value of debt and net present value of debt to exports ratio, end June 1997 (Mn $, %)*

Total net present value of debt	1,796
Multilateral	1,357
IDA	790
IMF	323
AfDF	101
AfDB	35
Other multilaterals	108
Bilateral	398
Paris Club	240
Non-Paris Club	146
Other	12
Arrears	41
Net present value of debt to exports ratio before assistance (%)	243
HIPC assistance (Mn $)	347
Net present value of debt to exports ratio after assistance (%)	196
(Exports of goods and non-factor services (Mn $)	739

Source: World Bank (1998a).

Between 1992 and 1993, there were a number of commercial debt buybacks and several debt reschedulings by the Paris Club. Debt worth US$ 100 million was rescheduled in 1992, and US$ 38 million in 1993, while debt reductions of about US$ 150 million were undertaken in the next two years. This meant that the government was able to marginally lower the total debt burden, as measured by the debt/exports ratio or the debt/GNP ratio. The stricter adherence to the stipulation that only concessional debt be incurred also helped keep the debt stock in check. However, this also meant that the share of multilateral debt in the total increased, with negative implications for the repayment options of the government.

In 1994, there was another increase in the debt stock, mainly as a result of rising multilateral loans. However, at the Paris Club meeting of February 1995, pre cut-off debt to the Paris Club was reduced by 67 per cent, the highest possible write-off. However, since the cut-off date is 1981, that is before Uganda's debt situation had escalated, the impact was not that dramatic on total debt. Only about US$ 50 million of it was written off. In terms of exports, the debt burden has fallen quite substantially in recent years, as the total export volume expanded.

The most dramatic change in the debt prospects has of course been the induction of Uganda into the Highly Indebted Poor Countries programme, as the first country to qualify on the basis of its strong macroeconomic performance. However, by 1996 Uganda's debt situation was no longer as serious, at least in the eyes of some observers, as had been the case at the initiation of the debate in the early 1990s that finally led to the HIPC. Still, Uganda's supporters argued that by delaying the country's qualification, the donor community would be punishing success instead of rewarding it, thereby sending the wrong signal to aid recipients.

Uganda reached "decision" point i.e. formal entry in the HIPC process in April 1997. The debt situation in NPV terms is set out in Table II.6 with the assumption of assistance under HIPC. The NPV value of total debt was US$ 1.8 billion in 1997, with the multilateral component comprising about 75 per cent. While the target for the Net Present Value of debt to exports ratio, after assistance under the programme, was set at 202 per cent (plus or minus 10 per cent points), the actual rate was 196 per cent i.e. 6 points below target. This should be compared to the estimated NPV of debt to exports without the HIPC initiative of 243 per cent. The outcome was better than expected for a number of reasons (mostly exogenous) such as better export performance, strength of US$ which lowered the value of debt stock denominated in other currencies. Following the completion point in April 1998, agreement was reached with almost all the country's multilateral creditors. The total amount of relief under HIPC is estimated at US$347 million in NPV terms (US$650 million in nominal terms), equivalent to a 20 per cent reduction of the debt stock, with 79 per cent of the relief from multilateral sources and the rest from bilateral ones. The initiative is expected to push the debt service ratio to below 20 per cent.

In nominal terms, the annual debt service reduction would be of the order of about US$ 30 million over a period of 25 years. This, the government has agreed, should be spent on the provision of social services. In fiscal 1998/99, the Poverty Action Fund (PAF), under which debt relief provided under the HIPC will be channelled to key services such as primary education, primary health care, water and sanitation, agricultural extension and rural/feeder roads, was launched.

In seeking to reduce the earlier accumulation of arrears a number of donors had helped form the "Fifth Dimension" which subsequently evolved (1996) into a multilateral debt fund (MDF). Money from the fund was then used to pay off debt owed to the World Bank and the IMF, thus ensuring that the adjustment programmes remained on track. The funds released domestically were then to be targeted to the social sectors. Ironically, this mechanism provided annual debt relief that, at about US$42 million in nominal terms, was slightly higher than that from HIPC. Yet, the MDF was not considered to be a long-term measure and is being wound up in 1999.

In a commentary, Collier (1996) contrasts the merits of three forms of aid delivery/use by comparing the MDF, the government's focus on infrastructure and social service expansion, and the alternative of using aid to defray the transaction costs of the private sector and thereby encourage its expansion. Collier finds the MDF alternative to be a low-risk, low-return strategy. The money is kept at the Bank of Uganda (as foreign reserves) when there might be more profitable uses of it in the rest of the economy. He is also sceptical of the government's ability to generate the high growth needed, given the still weak institutional structures and low absorption. The third alternative, which he favours, would imply lowering the overall tax burden on the private sector. He reckons that in less than a decade private-sector led growth would have been able to generate the exports and income streams necessary to meet the foreign exchange needs of the economy, enabling it to service debt.

Uganda has not accumulated a large domestic debt and the role of the treasury bills is still fairly limited. However, it has in recent years accumulated substantial domestic arrears, which have had a disruptive impact on macroeconomic aggregates because they are poorly structured and almost informal in character. In spite of the cash budget, the demand for extra budgetary resources has been high. The government and local authorities have issued promissory notes to domestic suppliers of goods and services. For example, these notes amounted to 48 billion shillings in fiscal 1996/97 falling to 20 billion in 1997/98 as the government insisted on departmental discipline. Total domestic arrears (excluding arrears to public enterprises) were estimated at 150 billion shillings, or 2.2 per cent of GDP, by the government in 1998.[8] The informal and short-term nature of these arrears has made their resolution difficult, enmeshed as they are in politics and with an element of collusion. However, there are also other arrears, for example those related to the demobilisation of soldiers in the early 1990s and even money owed to workers of the defunct East African Community. As part of its agreement with the IMF under the Enhanced Structural Adjustment Facility (ESAF), the

---

8. See letter dated 28 October 1998, from the Minister of Finance to the Managing Director, IMF.

government set up, in 1998, an Arrears Monitoring and Reporting Unit at the Ministry of Finance and Economic Planning with the view to eliminating domestic arrears within 3 years.

II.3.3. Conclusion

After the HIPC initiative, Uganda's debt situation is under a measure of control. However, there is a general feeling in government circles that the HIPC benefits fell well short of expectations. Still, unless there is a drastic economic decline, which should not be excluded in light of the dramatic worsening of the situation in the Great Lakes region, the debt service of the country should fall well within the country's export capacity. Exports are themselves projected to increase markedly over the medium to long term. To prevent fluctuations in policy, it is necessary to create debt management capacity at the Ministry of Finance and Economic Development and at the Bank of Uganda. A considerable part of the confusion in earlier years was a result of this lack of capacity. The debt relief made possible by the HIPC and other initiatives should benefit the poor people of Uganda by helping to extend services to the countryside. This is why the integrity of the PAF should be preserved. In this regard, the UPE project is well worth supporting with the funds released from the debt reduction.

Part III
Structural policies to promote long-run growth

III.1. Price policy and trade reform

III.1.1. Policy and non-policy barriers to trade

Though rapid reform had helped Uganda to reach a level of economic stability relatively quickly, trade reform has not been able to generate a rapid response in export production. Trade policy analysis often distinguishes between trade policy-induced and non-policy-induced barriers to trade. In Uganda, as noted above, much has been done to eliminate policy distortions, notably by allowing market forces to determine the level of the exchange rate and by removing price controls. Still, many policy-induced and institutional distortions have persisted, especially in the area of taxation, with the incidence of higher fuel taxation falling on exporters, since exporting in Uganda is transport intensive. Furthermore, the chaos in the financial sector has also increased the costs related to exporting activities, especially with respect to the dearth of credit or the unreliability of its supply. The non-policy barriers such as transport and freight costs are, however, more intractable. As a landlocked country, Uganda has higher transport costs than its neighbours, Kenya and Tanzania. This is not to say that the problem is beyond policy intervention. Indeed a well developed domestic network of roads and support structures could be effective in lowering transport costs (see Milner, Morrisey and Rudaheranwa, 1998). For example, recently the creation of a Mombasa-Kampala express cargo train service and removal of the need to unload merchandise at the border for customs purposes cut transport time to Kampala from two weeks to two days. Also lack of adequate refrigeration capacity at Entebbe Airport has impeded the expansion of horticultural exports.

In a recent paper, Richaud and Varoudakis (1999) look at factors, which have hindered the improvement of Africa's export competitiveness, thus preventing its integration into the world market (see also Rodrik, 1998). Focusing on the period 1985–1996, with data from countries representing all regions of the continent, they put the blame for Africa's poor export performance on the persistent misalignment of the real exchange rate, which itself depicts poor economic management, and excessively inward-oriented policies. The 1980s were characterised by rising budget deficits, two- to three-digit inflation levels, and fixed nominal exchange rates. Looking specifically at the period of intensified reforms, 1994–96, Richaud and Varoudakis note a sharp reduction in overvaluation, with increased openness in most parts of Africa. In Uganda, the liberalisation of the trade regime has had a strong impact on domestic competition, and thus on the efficiency of manufacturing firms (see Kasekende, Asea and Abuka, 1998). Notably, there has been a larger increase in technical efficiency for firms that produced import-competing goods than for those not competing in the international market. Trade liberalisation thus exposed firms to global competition, with beneficial effects on firm efficiency, an important factor in the country's attempts to integrate into the global economy.

III.1.2. Responses to changes in tariff structure and protection

The essence of Uganda's structural adjustment has been to lower trade barriers and expose the economy to global competition. Since the late 1980s, Uganda's trade regime has thus been gradually liberalised. An important step in trade liberalisation in the early 1990s was the abolition of the marketing boards for coffee, tea and cotton and their replacement by bodies that will focus on regulation and production support. As a first reaction to the liberalisation of the coffee market, over 100 private companies entered the coffee export market. Heightened competition improved the farm gate prices for coffee, which in turn boosted output. Also important, the Uganda Railways lost its monopoly on the transport of coffee to Mombasa, with other forms of transport coming in, again lowering transaction costs. Uganda was able to retake its position as Africa's premier producer of coffee. However, while price and market liberalisation had dramatic impacts on traditional exports, it is acknowledged that the response would have been greater, and that of the non-traditional exports more promising, were it not for lingering structural impediments, especially in the area of policy implementation.

Table III.1. *Indicators of trade liberalisation (%)*

	Average import tariff rate[a]	Average export tariff rate[b]	Non-traditional exports/GDP	Exports/GDP	Import/GDP	Trade openness[c]
1986	3	32	0.6	15	16	31
1987	5	14	0.9	11	20	31
1988	7	16	1.1	10	22	32
1989	8	8	1.2	9	22	31
1990	13	15	1.5	6	18	24
1991	19	9	1.5	5	12	17
1992	17	1	1.6	4	13	19
1993	23	0	2.0	5	14	19
1994	23	0	2.5	10	20	30
1995	24	2	3.4	11	21	32
1996	25	2	5.4	12	21	33

Note: a – (total value of tariff collected/total value of imports)100
b – (total value of export tax collected/total value of exports)100
c – ((exports+imports)/GDP)100
Source: Ssemogerere and Kalema (1998), p. 21.

Table III.1 shows some indicators of trade liberalisation in Uganda since 1986. In terms of tariff structures, Uganda has in the past few years reduced the number of tariff bands and gradually lowered the levels of tariff. In 1992, the tariff structure was in the range 10–60 per cent. The highest tariff rate had been reduced to 30 per cent by 1996 and to 20 per cent a year later. However, as a counterweight, especially in regional trade, an excise duty of 12 per cent was imposed on certain imports (notably textiles and manufactured foods). Lowered to 10 per cent in 1997, it was extended to most finished and consumption goods (see Morrisey and Rudaheranwa, 1998:7). However, import tariff collection has increased in recent years. Table III.1 shows that average nominal import tariff rates, calculated as tariff collection as a ratio of the value of total imports, have been rising, reaching 25 per cent in 1996. However, the increase in import duty receipts is partly due to the tightening of regulations, in a bid to eliminate discretionary exemptions from duty. Still, in fiscal 1996/97, discretionary exemptions accounted for US$26 million (see Morrissey and Rudaheranwa, 1998). The process of trade liberalisation is continuing, however. In the 1998 budget, the number of tariff bands was reduced to three of 0 per cent, 7 per cent and 15 per cent (Uganda, 1998a). Quantitative trade restrictions have essentially been eliminated. Only one, for tobacco, remains, to be removed in the course of 1999.

Exports as a per cent of GDP have not risen as fast as expected for a variety of reasons. Milner, Morrisey and Rudaheranwa (1998) argue that the implicit tax associated with transport costs in Uganda is quite high, and for many sectors exceeds the cost of trade policy barriers. If true, this indicates that Uganda faces a serious dilemma. Given its still narrow tax base, fuel taxation will continue to be important in generating government revenue. However, continuation of a high fuel tax policy will retard the expansion of the export sector. High transport costs do not only emanate from high fuel taxes: poor transport equipment and inadequate infrastructure also play a role. The Uganda government emphasis on road construction thus seems to be in tandem with the need to lower the costs of transport services. In attempting to compensate exporters for the costs of their inputs, the government instituted a duty drawback system. While it seems to have worked well for the bigger companies in the manufacturing sector, it has been less effective with respect to small-scale producers. The URA feels that the latter take too much time per amount of duty draw back assessed and thus the system has added to the administrative overload of the tax authorities.

A World Bank (1997) study has analysed the level of bias against exports in Uganda. They show that the effective rate of protection, measured as domestic prices with respect to the world market, was on average 93 per cent in 1994 or 64 per cent with regard to the regional market, while the ERP was -16 per cent for export sales. Export incentive schemes have generally been fairly ineffective in Africa, so lowering import tariffs may be one of the few instruments available to support export producers. An analysis of the effective rate of protection in Uganda's manufacturing industry was also undertaken with a view to assessing the impact on efficiency. Covering 61 firms, the analysis showed that 10 of the firms had negative value added at world prices and would eventually be eliminated under a liberal trade regime. However, two-thirds of the companies had a domestic resource cost (DRC) of less than one, implying that they would expand. The remaining eleven companies, however, had thrived under protection in the past and to survive they needed to respond to the increased competition, by becoming more efficient.

In their paper referred to above, Richaud and Varoudakis construct a "trade restrictiveness index" for six African countries (Burkina Faso, Côte d'Ivoire, Ghana, Mali, Tanzania, Uganda), included in the "emerging Africa" project, to assess the progress achieved towards trade liberalisation between 1985–96. Using the level of average tariffs on imports, as well as tariff dispersions and exemptions, four tariff regimes were identified: restrictive, relatively restrictive, moderate, relatively open and open. Non-tariff barriers such as quotas, bans, licensing schemes, foreign exchange allocation, government control on export and import marketing were used to classify regimes as restrictive, moderate and open. Finally, an overall index of trade restrictiveness was constructed: 1 indicating fully open and 10 indicating fully closed. In this evaluation Uganda is ranked together with Ghana and Mali, as a "strong reformer", with almost fully liberalised trade and foreign exchange markets. The three countries achieve a rating of between 3–4. However, Tanzania and Burkina, while scoring highly on the removal of non-tariff barriers, have an overall score of 5–6, mainly owing to still high tariff rates. They are thus only "moderate reformers". Finally, Côte d'Ivoire, which only began to see real reforms after the devaluation of the CFA franc in 1994, is considered a "slow reformer". Still these results can not predict the countries' real potential to generate exports, since this has a lot to do with the nature of the economy and its structure before the reforms were implemented. Thus ironically, although Côte d'Ivoire is considered a "slow reformer" in the above exercise, the reforms helped re-orient its sizeable industry, enabling a post-reform export boom.

III.1.3. Conclusion

In this section, we have looked at aspects of trade policy in Uganda and the extent to which previous reforms have helped create an atmosphere in which export activities can thrive. With respect to the removal of tariff and non-tariff barriers, Uganda seems to have performed better than its neighbours have. Its tariff rates are already lower than those of its partners in COMESA as well as in the reinstated East African Community. To prevent regional trade partners from taking advantage of this, the government has imposed an excise duty of 10 per cent on most import goods from the region. However, export growth has not been as rapid in Uganda as the pace of trade reform would suggest. There are indications that "geographical" and institutional barriers might be more serious than thought. Certainly the cost of transport is today so high as to render Uganda non-competitive in a whole range of goods, where she would reasonably have had comparative advantage. It is also feared that in the face of the erosion of preferences under the post-Lomé dispensation and well as the coming on stream of the free trade zones of COMESA and the East African Community, Uganda's export capacity risks further decline. In the circumstances, poorly functioning credit markets only serve to decrease Uganda's export potential. It is necessary for the government to start taking a serious look at the non-policy impediments of Uganda's trade regime and to devise ways of ameliorating them.

III.2. Strengthening the financial system

III.2.1. Introduction

The role of the financial sector in Uganda's recovery in the initial years was quite limited. Much of the earlier growth was due to the return of peace in the productive areas of the south, enabling farmers to resume activities. In other sectors of the economy, such as industry and infrastructure, a considerable amount of the investment or rehabilitation was thanks to increased donor inflows and the benefits of stabilisation. Moreover, since the financial sector was loaded with bad debts, its overall impact on growth and economic efficiency might well have been negative in the late 1980s. Still, for the growth process to be self-sustaining, there was need for an efficient financial sector, which was capable of providing a broad range of financial services. The years of decline saw the public revert to cash and barter for their daily transactions. The financial sector needed to win customers back.

The period of liberalisation has seen a surge in the activities of the financial sector in Uganda. At the start of the Economic Recovery Programme in 1987, the financial sector was dominated by government-owned institutions such as the Uganda Commercial Bank, Co-operative Bank and National Insurance Corporation. Moreover, the government had considerable stakes in the multinational banks, such as Barclays, Standard Chartered and Bank of Baroda. By 1998, however, the financial sector had expanded to a total of 20 commercial banks, 7 credit institutions, 28 insurance companies, 29 insurance brokerage firms, 2 development banks, 69 foreign exchange bureaux, a leasing company and close to one hundred NGOs focusing on micro finance (Uganda Manufacturers' Association, 1998). The country has also established a stock exchange as well as a capital markets authority. In many of the new institutions and sectors, the level of indigenous participation is fairly high.

III.2.2. Changes in financial sector policy

In 1992, the World Bank initiated a financial sector reform programme to address the negative features, resulting from the chaotic policies of the past, the goals being increased efficiency in the banking sector, financial deepening and broader responsiveness to customer needs. However, at the time, the sector was characterised by a number of serious shortcomings.

The government had created a number of non-bank financial institutions with the goal of extending credit to "key" sectors of the economy (i.e. agriculture and industry). However, defective collateral, insider or politically motivated lending and a poor legal system which impeded foreclosure decisions by the courts in cases of default, led to inefficient and, by the end of the 1970s, virtually insolvent financial institutions. Second, the commercial banking activities were overwhelmingly based in Kampala and dominated by the government-owned Uganda Commercial Bank (UCB) and Co-operative Bank (owned by co-operative unions and the government). Both banks were loaded with non-performing assets, some going back to the early 1970s but still on the books. Since the UCB was by far the largest single operator in the financial sector, with branches spread throughout the country, its insolvency meant that the whole economy was under threat. The misallocation of credit reduced the money available for productive investment and, to cover themselves, banks kept real interest rates unusually high. Ironically, the increase of donor money in the 1980s, which was channelled through and supervised by weak institutions such as the UCB and the Uganda Development Bank aggravated the size of the non-performing portfolio of the banking system.

The weak financial sector also made it impossible for the Bank of Uganda to pursue indirect monetary control measures in its management of monetary policy. In lieu of fine-tuning base money, the government was forced to impose tight controls on its expenditure and keep within programmed credit levels vis-à-vis the Bank of Uganda. The latter has also had to strengthen its role of bank supervisor. The crises of the late 1990s showed that far more management and technical skills were needed if the central bank was to be able to react to the rapid changes now taking place in Uganda's financial sector.

To address these problems, a number of policies were suggested: under a Financial Sector Adjustment Credit, the government has embarked on a number of policies aimed at rehabilitating and expanding the services provided by the sector. A 1993 Financial Sector Act was passed by Parliament and importantly it stipulates that the Bank of Uganda would supervise the financial sector and would have to be satisfied with the "competence and integrity" of the proposed management of a bank or financial company. Among other policy issues were the following:

1) To be allowed to operate banks had to meet all capital adequacy requirements.
2) Financial sector legislation had to be revised regularly in order to meet the demands of a rapidly changing economic environment.
3) The regulatory framework for the various parts of the financial sector: banks, insurance companies and capital markets needed to be strengthened.
4) As the overseer of the financial sector, the Bank of Uganda itself needed to be strengthened. There was need for a substantial re-capitalisation as well as a restructuring of its functions, notably that of bank supervision.

III.2.3. Structure of bank portfolios and interest rates

Macroeconomic policy outcomes have had important impacts on the financial sector in Uganda. The sector's response has in turn impacted on the overall economic environment. Table III.2 presents changes in the main interest rates in Uganda, 1991–98, where for purposes of comparison the rate of inflation is also presented. A surprising feature of interest rates in Uganda in recent years is the level of the real interest rate, which has continued to be high in spite of falling inflation and a declining discount rate of the Bank of Uganda. For example, the gap between the commercial bank rate and the rate of inflation has remained large throughout the 1990s. Thus while the Treasury bill rate was 31 per cent in 1991 compared to an inflation of 32.3 per cent, the commercial bank rate was as high as 44 per cent. In 1998 inflation was negative but lending rates were still above 20 per cent. A second feature is the unusually large spreads between returns on savings and the lending rates of the commercial banks. In 1991, the savings rate was 28 per cent, while the commercial bank rate was 12 per cent points higher. With declining inflation, banks have lowered savings rates to 3 per cent or below. In 1998, the commercial bank rate (at 20 per cent) was five times the savings rate.

Traditionally, the banking sector provided a more favourable rate for agriculture in the general belief that this would spur development. However, in recent years banks have been less willing (Table III.2) to extend cheap credit to farmers or agricultural projects, especially since the latter are riskier than others, and because given its plan to divest from the UCB, the government is unable to enforce this implicit subsidisation policy.

Table III.2. *Financial indicators: Treasury bill rates, interest rates and inflation 1991–98 (%)*

	1991	1992	1993	1994	1995	1996	1997	1998
Treasury bill, 91 days	31	49	24	11	7	11.8	9.8	7
Saving deposits	28	35	15	2	3	3.2	3.3	4.2
Maximum lending rate to agriculture	32	40	27	21.3	19.5	20.8	21.7	21.5
Bank of Uganda rediscount rate	38	43	25	19	10	14.1	12	10.2
Commercial bank rate	44	49	26	20	12	15.4	15.1	16.6
Inflation	32.3	66.3	-2.4	16	3.4	5.4	10.4	-1.35

Source: Bank of Uganda Files.

Table III.3 provides some figures on the distribution of commercial lending activities. We here compare 1991, roughly before the economy had fully stabilised, and 1997 when the government was looking for the means to sustain the underlying growth process. In the early 1990s, agriculture was still a target of commercial bank lending, especially since this was sanctioned by government. The major part of this was "crop financing", that is financing for the export of coffee. In 1991, close to a third of total loans and advances were made to agriculture. However, owing to high interest rates, coffee exporters have increasingly resorted to pre-export financing from abroad. Lending to agriculture had fallen to below 20 per cent by 1997. Not unexpectedly, the share going to trade and commerce has increased rapidly. While the share going to the sector was 39.2 in 1991, it had risen to about 50 per cent in six years. Trade and commerce has been a popular sector to finance because it has shown rapid growth during the era of liberalisation and also ensures rapid returns, with relatively little risk. The process can also be monitored fairly well via letters of credit to suppliers etc. which could all be handled by the creditor bank.

In contrast, manufacturing has not received as much credit as one would expect given the amount of emphasis it has had in recent years. In 1991, 11.7 per cent of total credit was received by the sector, rising to 21.7 in 1997. Many industrial projects have failed in the past, and financial sector operators are still wary of over committing themselves on a long-term basis in a still relatively risky environment.

Table III.3. *Commercial banks outstanding loans and advances to the private sector by type (% of total)*

Sector	1991	1997
Agriculture	33.6	19.2
Trade and commerce	39.2	50.5
Manufacturing	11.7	21.7
Transportation	8.0	3.1
Building and construction	7.3	5.3
Other	0.1	0.1

Source: Uganda (1998b).

Table III.4. *Proxies for financial vulnerability (billions of shillings and %)*

	1991	1992	1993	1994	1995	1996	1997
Foreign exchange reserves, shs.	38.8	85.7	134.2	212.6	375	507.9	663.9
Broad money (M2), shs.	138.7	212.6	301.8	402.6	504.4	609	705.6
Financial vulnerability (%)	28	40	44	52.8	74.3	83.4	94

Source: Uganda (1998b).

However, it would seem that the financial sector's vulnerability has seen some improvement in recent years. Given the assumption that in a liberalised economic environment residents may try to obtain foreign currency for their domestic currency holdings, we can measure financial vulnerability simply as the ratio between total foreign exchange reserves and the stock of broad money (M2). This is done in Table III.4. The vulnerability ratio was 28 per cent in 1991, implying that many actors would be caught short. By 1997, this ratio had risen to 94 per cent. Thus financial vulnerability had fallen by a factor of three. This is also reflected in Uganda's increasing (from a very low base) credit rating and rising domestic confidence. This parallels another measure of confidence, the months of imports that can be funded by the level of foreign reserves. The latter had risen to close to five months' worth of imports in late 1998.

III.2.4 Prospects and future challenges

During the last few years several new and relatively small banks have entered the market. These are controlled by a small group or a family and at times have close connections with powerful political factions. The owners of these banks often have vast business interests in other branches and seem to use the banks to finance these, and sometimes provide loans on dubious grounds. This has meant that some of the banks have very large stocks of non-performing assets. Most of the local banks have for a long time failed to make adequate provision for non-performing loans and also failed to satisfy capital adequacy requirements. The current minimum capital requirement for locally incorporated banks is UShs500 million that is less than half a million dollars. This seems much too low and there were plans for raising it substantially in 1998.

The mushrooming of weak banks has increased the fragility of the financial sector and its susceptibility to shocks, both internal and external. Recent experience in Uganda has shown that the impact of a bank's collapse can be larger than its market share. The failure in September 1998 of the International Credit Bank and the Trust Bank (the Ugandan branch of a Kenyan bank) and "temporary" closure of the TransAfrica Bank, all in the course of a single week, shook the whole of the financial sector. However, the three affected banks account for less than 5 per cent of total bank deposits in Uganda!

Is it necessary to advocate the growth of indigenous institutions even at the risk of falling efficiency? Are indigenous banks inherently weak? The answer given by their advocates is no. Still, indigenous banks have serious drawbacks: they are new, small and lack reputation. Many individuals rushed into the banking sector in recent years with little or no previous training or experience in finance or in how to run a bank. Ownership and management functions are poorly delineated, while efficiency is often subjugated to compassion. Notably, relatives with little specialist experience in banking sit on the boards, all with a view to keeping "things" in the family. In times of economic turbulence, it is difficult for clients to distinguish between a disparate array of small banks, making it difficult for indigenous banks to establish a reputation.

Ultimately, however, the reputation of the banks cannot be much better than the quality of their borrowers. In Uganda, the modern sector elite i.e. those demanding "profitable" banking services, though expanding, is still very small. Smaller still is the financial elite. There is thus considerable scope for inbreeding and recycling of ideas, that is borrowers and lenders might be one and the same. A notable outcome has been the failure, even after the recent economic reforms, to isolate politics from finance—that is to keep politicians from being policymakers and patrons at the same time. This type of system creates inefficiencies, which tend to constrain economic growth. The same problems have for a long time been observed in Kenya, where the consequences were analysed by Bigsten and Moene (1996).

While politicians, like other economic actors, demand credit, a number of attributes tend to make them riskier borrowers. They tend to borrow on the strength of their political tenure, which invariably is shorter than the time needed to pay off their loans. However, they often possess "high-powered" incentives mainly connected to their knowledge of the workings of the system. Small banks, often indigenous, are thus often put in a difficult situation. Loans are given without adequate analysis or evaluation of risks or of the security of collateral. Nor is there an adequate cash flow analysis or insistence on a realistic business plan. The banking system has been weakened by large loans given by these local banks to influential individuals or to firms owned by the owners of the banks. The fact that there are loans given to people in high places has also made it harder for the Bank of Uganda to act decisively. The politicians are straddling: they have one foot in politics and another in business. They then exploit this double role for own benefit. Given the still small size of the "independent" private sector, it is difficult to establish an effective countervailing force against these anomalies. Once loans have been made, politicians, or groups allied to them, do not feel obliged to repay. A large portion of the many assets, mainly dwellings, repossessed by the Non-Performing Assets Recovery Trust (NPART), created by the government to recover loans, indicates the scale of the problem.

But even "ordinary" borrowers have been a problem. For example, a number of micro-finance projects have been created in the past decade to serve the informal sector and farmers in the countryside, that is the needs of those at the lower end of the income distribution. These projects have not performed better than those in the formal sector. Collateral has again been a particularly difficult issue. It is often in the form of land or real estate, located upcountry and thus in effect much less valuable than the acquired loan.

The capital market in Uganda is very poorly developed at present. The Capital Market Authority, started in 1996, has been instrumental in the creation of a legal framework for the financial sector and the creation of a market for financial instruments. The Kampala Stock Exchange (KSE) started activities in January 1998 by launching the East African Development Bank bond. Shortly afterwards, the PTA Bank launched its bond as well. So far there are no other shares trading on the exchange, although there are a few privatised firms in the pipeline. The delay has been blamed on government for what might be the wrong reason. The Capital Markets Authority has asked the government to consider waiving its full disclosure and proper accounting stipulations in order to allow companies, who by implication had defaulted on these matters, to register with the stock exchange. If the purpose of the stock exchange is to raise transparency in business operations lenience of this nature could set bad precedent, especially if authorities begin by relaxing the very rules supposed to enhance credibility.

Still, something has to be done to get activities going on the Stock Exchange. Authorities could borrow a leaf from the book of Kenya's Finance Minister and introduce an "amnesty bond" or a similar instrument, which would enable companies to come clean on their undeclared incomes. However, a point on which the government could be brought to task is the rather poor sequencing of the privatisation and the introduction of the stock exchange. The government could have used the stock exchange in its privatisation of some of the parastatals. This would have helped spread ownership, at least initially, and would have created opportunities for learning by doing for the now relatively idle machinery around the stock exchange. With hindsight, the insistence on having a "strategic investor" has not worked well, as the experience of the Uganda Commercial Bank and the Nile Hotel has shown. These should be targets for privatisation via the stock exchange.

Is the stock exchange the ultimate source of investment in the future? The government seems to believe that it is. In actual fact, as a recent World Bank survey (1995) indicated, most companies in Uganda still rely on retained savings or owners' capital injections for capital accumulation. This seems to be the case in many developed countries as well. Still, a stock exchange market is important in developing countries as a signalling instrument and one to help raise transparency in financial matters and in business in general. When it works well, the stock exchange ensures that companies are owned by a broader spectrum of the population. However, ownership and control are not the same thing. A thinly spread ownership structure might mean that no group has real power over the company. There is no authority to manage the often demanding post-privatisation restructuring that is needed. When ownership is thinly spread, as via the stock exchange, owners cannot exercise power by seeking to have changes made in the company. Their only option is to sell shares and exit. They thus vote with their feet. Owners that really want to restructure companies and make them profitable also like to have their opinions heard. They want voice. There is thus tension between the need to broaden ownership and that of effective corporate governance.

III.2.5 Conclusion

Uganda's experience indicates that if not remedied, the currently poor performance of its financial sector threatens the progress made in other sectors of the economy. There is need for the development of a new bank culture to match the increasingly market-oriented nature of the economy. Under the increasingly globalised nature of the economy, banks need to devise systems that enable them to lend profitably once again and their clients to borrow responsibly. A system based on the presumption of a high rate of default cannot be good for the development of the financial sector or the economy.

The development of the financial sector is closely linked to that of market development. The Ugandan experience shows that mere change of ownership was not going to transform indigenous banks overnight into efficient producers of financial services. Best practices had to be encouraged by drawing experienced operators from elsewhere and raising the level of competition. The question of industry standards was also bound to be crucial. While Uganda has set up regulations for the running of the financial sector, this can only produce results if the regulations are enforceable. There must also be clear rules of entry, exit and general conduct. It might even be necessary to encourage banks to set up mechanisms for self-regulation, and to encourage transparency. Finally, banks must also be encouraged to specialise. This would be the best way of profiling their activities. Good reputations will only come when banks achieve a level of excellence in service delivery via increased professionalism and profitability.

III.3. Investing in infrastructure and social overhead capital

III.3.1. Introduction

In the first decade of independence, the public sector's involvement in the provision of social services in Uganda was fairly extensive backed up by a performing economy. Education and primary health care were given considerable emphasis, seen as instruments that would help reduce ignorance and disease in the countryside, and boost overall economic development. Partly with donor support, a rapid expansion of health and education services was undertaken in the first years of independence, accompanied by impressive private sector initiative in both areas. A considerable emphasis was also placed on infrastructure development, with the government expanding the basic services left at independence. However, the rapid population growth and the onset of crisis in the 1970s began to depress the supply and quality of social services (Heyneman, 1979).

In a recent evaluation (African Development Bank, 1998), Africa's slow growth, relative to the countries of East Asia for example, has been blamed on its poor level of human capital development and inferior rate of accumulation of "infrastructure" capital. The chaotic policies and civil wars in the various countries have prevented the development of effective institutions. These factors have probably been more marked in Uganda than elsewhere.

Four problems have been associated with the poor delivery of infrastructure and social services in Uganda. First, the overriding problem has been the inability of the central and local governments to provide adequate resources. Second, the institutions set up by the government for training, regulation and research gradually fell into disrepair. Third, the financial constraints reduced the levels of remuneration in the service sector, notably the pay for civil servants and teachers, to intolerable levels. Government workers became lethargic. Fourth, the provision of social and infrastructure services in Uganda has been plagued by an urban bias. Modern services, roads and telecommunications are concentrated in the confines of the major urban centres. There is a shortage of resources and personnel to modernise and adapt the institutions to the needs of the rapidly expanding population.

However, it has not been easy for policymakers to determine where the limited resources should be focused. For example, whether to provide a cheap or even free basic education to the broad masses or to concentrate more on the higher levels of education in order to improve manning capacity (Opio-

Odong, 1993). Similarly, the government has swayed between the need for primary health care, as opposed to carrying on within the large, expensive and bureaucratic hospital structures. In the 1990s, with market reforms firmly entrenched, the government has had to decide what level of participation it wished to maintain in service and infrastructure provision, and also how to ensure that the vulnerable groups were protected.

III.3.2. Human capital

Education

The education sector in Uganda comprises a fairly large number of schools and colleges. The three Rs (writing, reading and arithmetic) were popularised at the turn of the century by rival Catholic and Protestant missionaries, and mission-built institutions remain at the core. At the very top of Uganda's educational infrastructure is Makerere University. The first years of independence saw the construction of a number of primary and secondary schools, in diverse areas of the country (Odaet, 1990; Nsibambi, 1976)—for example, in the course of 1964, 25 secondary schools were started or upgraded for government support.

With the fall of government revenue in the 1970s and increases in military expenditure, the state was no longer able to expand education. The sector went into deep crisis, for close to two decades. On taking over power in 1986, the NRM government had wished to see rapid social sector improvements. Hoping for a rapid economic recovery, government had promised in the 1987/88-budget speech to assume a larger share of the costs of basic education. For primary education, the government was to cover 50 per cent of the costs, while for secondary schools it was to cover between 65 and 75 per cent. This fell through in the subsequent years as the government was confronted with military incursions in the various parts of the country.

Table III.5. *Parents'/government contribution to primary school income 1991–95 (%)*

Year	Parents	Government
1991	75	25
1992	75	25
1993	67	33
1994	57	43
1995	55	45

Source: Ablo and Reinikka (1998).

Before the introduction of universal primary education in 1997, which saw primary school enrolment rise to 95 per cent, there was a real fear about the evolution of a dual system of education. The children of the affluent would find their way to the better schools via better training at the lower levels, enabled by better PTA contributions, while the rest made do with the largely makeshift structures in the private sector or on a self-help basis. The availability of funds also affects the quality of feeding in schools, with poorer schools skipping feeding programmes altogether (Oundo and Burton, 1992). In recent years, the government has tried to curtail the influence of the PTAs, though lack of funds prevents it from establishing an effective alternative. Table III.5 based on a study by Ablo and Reinikka (1998) shows that parents met over 50 per cent of school incomes (for all practical purposes running expenses) for the first half of the 1990s, via regular fees and PTA levies. The government's share has been creeping up slowly, and reached a peak in 1997 when partial universal primary education was declared

As Table III.6 shows, education attainment in Uganda has a gender as well as a regional bias. Urban populations and those in the southern parts of the country, with proximity to government services have attained high levels of education while those in the periphery are poorly educated.

According to data from the Planning and Statistical Unit of the Ministry of Education, primary level enrolment was 1.3 million in 1980 (43 per cent females) rising to 2.5 million by 1989 (45 per cent females). This marked an average growth rate of 22 per cent per year, way ahead of that of the population. This rapid improvement was a result of the much increased enrolment ratio, partly enabled by improved security. In secondary school, total enrolment was 73,092 in 1980 (30 per cent females) increasing three-fold to 238,500 in 1989 (45 per cent females). Although the increase in the number of females attending secondary school was marked towards the end of the 1980s, the ratio of females enrolled in the various institutions, especially the technical ones, is still far below that of males.

Table III.6. *Uganda 1995: Level of educational attainment by region and sex (%)*

	Women			Men		
	No education	Primary	Secondary and over	No Education	Primary	Secondary and over
Urban	10.6	49.8	39.7	5.4	37.5	57.2
Rural	34.1	57	8.9	12.6	67.3	20.1
Central	14.4	62.0	23.6	9.7	52.3	38
Eastern	29.6	58.4	12.0	12.2	65.1	22.7
Northern	47.6	46.0	6.5	9.8	69.3	20.9
Western	35.6	54.8	9.5	14.7	68.1	17.2
Average	30.6	56	13.5	11.6	63.1	25.3

Sources: Uganda (1996b), Demographic and Health Survey, 1995.

Regional disparities are also reflected in the achievement of subsequent cohorts since parents with high education tend to ensure that their children also attain a good education. In the early 1990s, primary school enrolment was only about 66 per cent nationally, but with wide regional variation. For example, while 9 out 10 children attended primary school in Kampala and surrounding areas, in the late 1980s, only 2.4 in 10 did so in Moroto, in the north western part of the country. In secondary schools, enrolment was 11 per cent, indicative of the high dropout rate, especially for girls. In primary school the teacher/pupil ratio is 1 to 35 while in secondary schools it is 1 to 20. However,

with few opportunities for side incomes and shortage of basic services in the
countryside, rural schools found it very difficult to recruit teachers.

Table III.7. *Uganda: Education statistics 1989–1997 (numbers)*

	Primary schools	Secondary schools	Primary teachers	Secondary teachers	University teachers	Primary enrolment	Secondary enrolment	University enrolment
1989	7,684	508	81,418	12,919	573	2,532,800	238,467	5,405
1990	7,667	510	81,590	11,069	579	2,281,590	223,498	5,746
1991	8,046	512	78,259	13,476	574	2,539,549	235,245	7,468
1992	8,325	509	86,821	14,660	876	2,364,078	226,805	10,090
1993	8,430	508	91,905	14,620	1,060	2,462,309	231,430	7,529
1994	8,442	567	84,043	16,245	1,154	2,508,692	246,698	8,051
1995	8,531	519	76,151	14,447	955	2,636,409	255,048	11,469
1996	8,550	619	82,600	18,500	847	2,737,334	289,506	11,848
1997	10,452	619	98,700	18,696	Na	5,303,564	336,022	14,857

Source: Uganda (1998b): Statistical Abstract 1998, p. 108.

Table III.7 presents some basic statistics on education in Uganda covering the
period 1989–97. The demand for education has increased in the past few years
with rising enrolments in both primary and secondary schools. The construction of structures has also expanded although at a lower pace. This implies
increased overcrowding in many schools. However, there is concern that the
number of teachers in the various institutions has not risen by much. Thus the
capacity for Ugandan schools to impart learning skills might still be weak.
The government recently introduced a system of (nearly) Universal Primary
Education, with four children from each family attending school free. Enrolment in primary education went up by 80 per cent in 1997, with class sizes
increasing by over 50 per cent in some cases. The education budget has increased substantially, although a recent evaluation by Ablo and Reinikka
(1998) suggests that higher budgetary numbers have yet to translate into ob-
servable improvements in service delivery. Still, to contend with the increased
school attendance, the government will have to provide more resources to the
education sector, and probably reduce allocations to others if the macroeconomic economic stability attained by the country is not to be jeopardised.

In 1987, the government set up an Education Policy Review Commission
(EPRC) to look at all aspects of the country's educational structure. A government white paper on Implementation and Recommendations was released
in 1992 for general discussion and was subsequently tabled in Parliament.
There are four main innovations: first, primary school would be extended by
one year from 7 to 8 years. Since students leaving primary school will be
somewhat older, this would enable an increased vocationalisation of education to the benefit of those who might not be able to continue. Second, the cost
of education at the primary level would be lowered. This would be done in
stages, but with the ambition of universal primary education by the year 2010.
Third, there would be increased emphasis on gender equity in education.
Attempts would also be made to provide all schools with adequate facilities
for girls. Fourth, government would seek to allocate at least 20 per cent of its

budgetary resources to education. This can be compared to the 11 per cent share of education in total expenditure in the 1993/94 budget and 4 per cent in 1991/92.

Health

Uganda's health status is poorer than that of other countries at its level of per capita income, reflecting in large measure the persistence of the effects of civil war and the institutional disruptions of the past decades. The impact of the AIDS pandemic has also been disastrous for the country's health sector, given the public sector's poor resource base. In line with the other services, the physical condition of Uganda's health institutions deteriorated enormously in the 1970s and the 1980s. In 1986, the value of the public health budget was less than 10 per cent that of the early 1970s. In fact in the early 1990s the govern-ment was spending only about US$ 4 per capita, and year, on health care, compared to double that in neighbouring Kenya and over US$30 in Botswana. In the mid-1990s, Uganda had close to 1,400 health institutions of which 60 per cent were government owned. At about 100 hospitals, the country had over 200,000 people per hospital. With the collapse of the primary health care system in the 1980s, mortality from diarrhoea infections, malaria and malnu-trition increased.

Table III.8. *Uganda 1995: Distance to nearest facility providing health services (%)*

	Antenatal care		Immunisation	
	Urban	Rural	Urban	Rural
< 1 km	37.2	9.6	24.3	9.8
1–4 km	59.9	31.5	71.9	37.3
5–9 km	2.2	30.7	2.2	29.2
10–14 km	0.0	13.6	0.9	11.8
15–29 km	0.0	9.4	0.0	6.5
30+ km	0.0	3.1	0.0	3.2

Source: Uganda (1996b): Demographic and Health Survey, 1995.

Table III.8 shows that access to institutions varies greatly between rural and urban regions (which also implies disparities between rural regions near the centre and those at the periphery). For example the majority of mothers in urban centres have access to antenatal care and immunisation within four kilometres of their residence, with about a quarter within just a kilometre of a health care providing institution. In rural areas, on the other hand distances to health centres are much longer. Given poor transport, and lower incomes, some rural dwellers chose not to seek modern medical treatment. These prob-lems of access thus tend to cement the wide rural differences in health status, which in turn reflects on livelihoods.

It was also shown by the Demographic and Health Survey (Uganda, 1996b) that the maternity care women receive is crucial to infant and child survival. For the period 1991–95, infant mortality was on average 81 per 1,000 live births. However, under-fives mortality was as high as 147 per 1,000 live births. Urban infant mortality was 74.4 compared to 87.6 for rural areas, while corresponding figures for under-fives mortality were 133.5 and 159.1, respectively. However, the Northern and Eastern regions, where civil war and economic disruption persisted, had infant mortality rates of close to 100 per 1,000 live births and also much higher levels than average for under-fives mortality.

The government has made some attempts to revive health services. A major achievement was the successfully executed immunisation program, which had reached more than 50 per cent of the pre-school children by the early 1990s. This seems to have had some positive effect on infant mortality. Another has been the rehabilitation of the main health institutions, notably Mulago, with help from foreign donors.

But as in much of Sub-Saharan Africa, a major constraint on the provision of health services is the low level of salaries for employees in the system. The low morale that results leads to negligence, absenteeism and theft. As in education, there is also a wide disparity in the availability and quality of health services between urban and rural areas. To fill the vacuum left by the poor performance and inadequacy of government institutions, a number of private clinics were set up in urban areas. In rural areas, households resorted to local herbs for treatment. It has been noted (Kayizzi-Mugerwa, 1993) that the mushrooming of health clinics has not necessarily improved the health status of the urban population. Lacking an enforceable policy on drugs, the country has in recent years seen deterioration in general resistance partly a by-product of hurried medical diagnosis and inadequate prescriptions.

On assuming power in 1986, the NRM set up a Health Policy Review Commission to look into all matters pertaining to the health sector. Its work was completed in September 1987, with its recommendations forming the basis for a National Health Policy. The issues to be resolved were: first, the health delivery system had to be made more efficient; second, it had to be affordable; and third, it had to reach as many people as possible, especially since it was estimated that the current system only reached 45 per cent of the population. Overall, the government's health budget was extremely lopsided, the bulk (about 80 per cent) went to hospitals, mainly Mulago in Kampala. Primary health care got a very small portion of the available resources.

Since the thrust of the current system has been curative rather than preventive, the availability of drugs has been crucial to its functioning. However, Uganda has a poor drugs culture characterised by massive phoney demand. Lack of a drug administration and licensing policy has led to shortages of crucial drugs but to an apparent excess supply of others, given the proliferation of drug stores. The Uganda Essential Drugs Management Programme, supported by donors, alleviated the immediate shortages of key drugs but the prospects remained precarious and the health sector continued to be underfunded in the 1980s. Hospitals and other institutions with their own private funds, such as those controlled by religious missions, managed to offer good quality services at reasonable cost. In a bid to reduce the persistent shortages, policymakers have devised a number of cost sharing schemes. There have been four main arguments for cost sharing (see UNICEF, 1994; Kaheru, 1990; Van der Heijden and Jitta, 1993). The first is that it reduces the burden on government. Second, that a bigger resource envelope would increase scope for innovation, flexibility and delivery. Third, that resource availability would help increase remuneration of health service workers. Fourth, that with decentralisation, cost sharing would enable communities to take greater responsibility for service delivery.

However, a number of fears have been voiced. Social services are not amenable to the type of competition seen in the business sector. Patients fear that the introduction of cost sharing would fail to eliminate the "informal fees" that they were paying to social sector workers. They would be doubly taxed. In its recommendations, a Task Force on Health Financing (Uganda, 1990a) suggested that the money collected via cost sharing was to be retained locally and to be used in the following 3–4 years, at least, to motivate staff. This, however, fell through in the political process, partly owing to infighting between ministries. It is also possible that the extent of foreign financing was so huge, for example in the 1990/91 financial year external funding of the health sector amounted to 61 per cent of total outlays, 80 per cent capital and 55 per cent recurrent, that the government did not feel compelled to undertake unpopular reforms. Still, several local administrations introduced their own schemes to collect money, which they use to improve wages for their staff.

However, examples cited by the UNICEF (1994:39) indicate that the improvements in wages resulting from cost sharing, may not be sufficient to improve morale in the health service sector. In the suburbs of Kampala cost sharing did not appear to have improved performance, although there was a short-term drop in patient load on its introduction. In contrast, work morale seemed to have improved in the up-country institutions where cost sharing was introduced, notably in Arua. It would seem, therefore, that due to the availability of alternative income sources, Kampala health workers would need much higher incentive packages before a change in their work patterns is observed.

Budgets and reality

Discussion of social expenditure raises the issue of how closely related budget allocations are to the reality on the ground. Ablo and Reinikka (1998) sought to resolve this question by investigating, using a specially designed survey for the purpose, whether the budgets allocated to social services in Uganda actually affected service provision at the local level. In spite of rapid increases in social and sector expenditure outlays, for example, resources to basic services, including primary education had increased, as well as those to agricultural extension, feeder roads, primary education and health care, official figures on outcomes were not reflecting sufficient improvements. Their query was "do budgets matter" if governments are not efficient at delivering public services?

Using field survey data for 19 districts, covering 250 government aided schools and 100 health clinics and collecting data for the period 1991–95, they found that even fewer resources reached the lower levels than was generally anticipated. That the levels of enrolment might have gone up in the period of study was mainly due to the return of peace and the role of the parents in funding education. In health, the problems of health workers "privatising" the system persisted, with increased outlays having little impact on decreasing the cost of health care. Their conclusion is that budgets in countries with still weak institutions matter less than more serious efforts put in place to ensure the provision of at least a minimum level of services, especially in the countryside. In other words, while the governments might, by raising the budgetary allocation to basic services, placate donors this will not, on its own, ensure that resources are delivered to the population.

III.3.3. Physical infrastructure

In the 1980s, Uganda's infrastructure was a constraint on growth because of its poor quality and slow pace of rehabilitation. In the 1990s, however, there have been major efforts to rehabilitate the infrastructure, although in light of the rapidly expanding economy this has proven inadequate. It has been argued that in early to medium stages of development the growth in the demand for basic infrastructure, including power generation, transport and communications, telecommunications, irrigation and agricultural extension services, often far exceeds the growth of the economy itself. This implies that infrastructure bottlenecks arise, becoming a drag on economic growth even as the population begins to enjoy the benefits of rapid growth. Hirschman (1958) argued that to overcome these constraints it is necessary to accumulate an excess of "social overhead capital". This would serve as something of a generalised subsidy to producers, lowering costs of production across the board. For many countries in Africa, however, constructing excess overhead capital has not been possible since infrastructure expansion has received low priority since the economic crises of the 1970s.

The term "infrastructure" is far from a homogeneous product concept. For example, though roads and airports provide transport services, they operate under quite different environments. Similarly, while water-engineering techniques might be common to irrigation services as well as to electricity generation, the two are only vaguely related in practice. However, seen as an amenity to producers and consumers, infrastructure provision has implications for production decisions as well as for labour markets.

On the production side, the size and quality of infrastructure provision affects variable as well as fixed costs. An increase in variable costs, arising for example from the impact of poor infrastructure on transport costs, reduces the scale of production, but also directly affects the firm's price-setting decisions. On the other hand, the effect on fixed costs changes the profit-maximising level of output. In responding to the relative price shifts caused by, for example, malfunctioning infrastructure, the factor intensities of firms are bound to change. Firms might become capital or labour intensive depending on their possibilities for factor substitution and the market situation. Furthermore, since infrastructure availability impacts on profitability, and thus the long-term viability of the firm, it influences the firm's localisation decision. Firms will thus locate in regions or countries where "certain conditional thresholds" with regard to infrastructure supply are met. This in turn influences the spatial distribution of domestic industrial activity, in effect determining the size of the industry as well as its employment capacity (Hulten and Schwab 1991).

In 1994, the World Bank undertook a survey of private sector enterprises in Uganda, with a view to identifying the constraints affecting their expansion and general operation. One of the areas focused being that of infrastructure. In Tables III.9 and III.10 tabulations of firm responses to questions regarding how they were affected by infrastructure availability are presented. Respondents were asked to indicate the severity of the infrastructure constraint by assigning values ranging from 1, when the particular infrastructure type was not a problem, to 5 when it was a serious problem. The designation infrastructure included space for doing business, power supply, telecommunications, water supply, waste disposal, commercial truck transport, roads, railways, seaports and airports.

Table III.9 presents firm responses to infrastructure constraints by size of the firm, with the latter determined by the total number of employees. Five size groups were identified: micro firms, with 1–5 employees, small (6–20), medium (21–50), large (50–100), and very large (over 100). The results indicate that electricity provision is the most serious constraint on firm performance across all size groups. Regarding power breakdowns, all firms score above 3, while the bigger ones reach a score of 4, implying rising severity with firm size. Voltage fluctuations are also a serious problem, again affecting larger firms more severely than smaller ones. A number of firms reported heavy losses owing to loss of equipment as a result of the power fluctuations, while others were not able to meet delivery deadlines as a result. Another problem, not explicitly addressed by the questionnaire, was the high cost of connection to the mains for new firms as well as the delays before power was delivered. These have proven to be serious impediments to business growth.

Telecommunications, notably telephones, were also a serious problem. Table III.9 indicates that, as in the case of electricity, problems with communications were more serious for bigger companies. The latter do a considerable amount of business on the phone, including the procurement of inputs and spares from abroad. Firms were not generally too constrained by lack of water, systems for waste disposal or railway transport. This was not because these services were performing particularly well, but because firms had found their own means of ensuring adequate water supply, by for example building water tanks, or meeting the costs of connection to the water mains. Many firms have also taken to dumping waste, with serious implications for the future. With regard to roads, it is again noteworthy that the bigger firms are more affected than the smaller ones, they simply have much more to transport. Poor access to markets is costly for all firms, but more so for the bigger ones. With the economic recovery, many companies are looking beyond Uganda's borders at regional markets. Exporting, while lucrative, is very vulnerable to poor roads since delays raise transport costs.

Table III.9. *Infrastructure constraints on private firms by size, 1994*
(average scores: 1=no obstacle, 5=severe obstacle)

	Micro (1-5) n=46	Small (6-20) n=86	Medium (21-50) n=72	Large (50-100) n=26	Very large (over 100) n=35	Average Score
Lack of land or space	2.77	2.45	2.65	2.65	2.45	2.58
Power breakdown	3.28	3.54	3.30	3.85	4.00	3.52
Power fluctuations	3.05	2.90	2.71	3.31	3.68	3.02
Telecommunications	2.82	2.76	2.75	3.07	3.05	2.84
Water supply	2.35	2.34	2.40	2.42	2.57	2.40
Waste disposal	2.08	1.92	1.91	1.76	1.88	1.93
Industrial waste disposal	2.20	1.89	1.90	2.42	2.44	2.07
Commercial transport	1.42	1.84	2.29	2.04	2.03	2.00
Roads	2.28	2.28	2.87	2.96	3.45	2.67
Railway transport	1.23	1.67	1.79	1.77	2.03	1.75
Ports and shipping	1.00	1.45	1.60	2.03	2.65	1.72
Air freight services	1.07	1.59	1.65	2.00	2.44	1.76

Source: World Bank: Uganda Private Enterprise Survey, 1994.

Table III.10. *Infrastructure constraints on private firms by sector, 1994*
(average scores: 1=no obstacle, 5=severe obstacle)

	Industry n=75	Agro- industry n=34	Commerce n=53	Services n=76	Con- struction n=27	Average Score
Lack of land or space	2.80	2.47	2.34	2.67	2.33	2.58
Power breakdown	3.37	3.65	3.56	3.60	3.48	3.52
Power fluctuations	3.01	2.90	2.94	3.08	3.20	3.02
Telecommunications	3.01	3.12	2.42	2.85	2.77	2.84
Water supply	2.51	2.56	2.21	2.43	2.18	2.40
Waste disposal	1.98	1.67	1.90	2.03	1.81	1.93
Industrial waste disposal	2.11	2.32	1.94	1.97	2.20	2.07
Commercial transport	2.42	2.27	1.71	1.59	2.16	2.00
Roads	3.13	2.96	2.14	2.27	3.15	2.67
Railway transport	2.01	1.75	1.52	1.40	2.28	1.75
Ports and shipping	2.28	1.55	1.46	1.27	1.95	1.72
Air freight services	2.24	1.46	1.54	1.47	1.87	1.76

Source: World Bank: Uganda Private Enterprise Survey, 1994.

Table III.10 presents the responses by sector of origin. Though the infrastructure impacts are given a slightly different dimension, electricity problems are still the most serious constraint on economic activities. Telecommunication constraints are more serious in manufacturing (industry and agro-industry) than in commerce, services and construction. This reflects on the nature of the manufacturing activity, with the need for constant contact with the markets for inputs and produce. Poor roads also have a much more serious impact on manufacturing, with a score of around 3, while construction is also seriously affected. The latter case is because construction work demands the transport of both heavy equipment and materials to and from the construction site. With regard to waste disposal, manufacturing firms as well as those in construction register a higher level (though not serious) of inconvenience than firms in other sectors. This pattern is repeated with respect to the various types of transport for goods and services.

In the course of the 1990s, the government has tried to respond to demands for improved infrastructure services. A general rehabilitation and extension of the electricity generation at Jinja has been going on for the past five years and is nearing completion. It is expected that this will increase power supply and minimise the current disruptions. There are also a number of other power projects on stream, including the construction of a large dam along the Nile by a private company. A Norwegian group has also embarked on the construction of a dam in northern Uganda that will greatly alleviate power shortages in that part of the country. Uganda seems to have a comparative advantage in power generation and should, therefore, be able to become an important regional electricity supplier.

III.3.4 Conclusion

The long period of chaos and decline in Uganda left the social sectors in extremely poor condition. Primary education was only possible thanks to high fees and compulsory PTA contributions. Those who could not afford it or those in areas engulfed by civil war failed to take their children to school at all. A similar disruption was apparent in the health sector. Services in government institutions had collapsed, while private sector initiatives were inadequate. The reforms of the past decade have seen a revival in service provision and the newly declared UPE seems to have had a positive impact on school attendance, even for poor households. Yet, the rising share of the social sectors in the budget should have had a larger impact on the ground. It is thus important to devise measures to ensure better service delivery at the local level. This demands improvements in the resource delivery functions in line ministries as well as strengthened accountability. However, although there was a general decline in social service provision in Uganda, it was more marked in the countryside. The improvement of rural services and infrastructure will thus be important in attempts to bring the benefits of reform to the rest of the country.

Part IV
Public sector management and economic performance

IV.1. Securing the private/public sector boundary

IV.1.1. Introduction

When nationalisation was started in the late 1960s, the focus was on "strategic" sectors such as mining, beverages, banking and textiles. However, the sense of what was "strategic" changed with the political demands. Details of today's privatisation programme indicate that the government had gone well beyond the original intention of state ownership i.e. to promote rapid growth and ensure income equality. Thus firms recently reprivatised not only include those in textiles, cement, and transport but also cinemas, hotels, food oils and tourist agencies. Clearly "strategic" was merely a euphemism for total economic control.

However, in many cases, governments were forced to subsidise the activities of nationalised companies, directly or by reducing their tax liabilities. These "soft budget" constraints encouraged waste and obstructed the flow of services, such as water, electricity, roads, and railways and harbours. Thus public firms became a major cause of fiscal imbalance.

IV.1.2. Privatisation

The privatisation of state property in Uganda has led to a lively debate. The proceeds of a recent seminar on privatisation for Ugandan MPs at Entebbe suggest that while legislators generally considered privatisation a *fait accompli*, they were worried about how little influence they, and by analogy their constituents, had had on the process.

Three major issues have arisen from the privatisation debate. The first and most obvious relates to the question of ownership. The private-public ownership debate has been superseded by the foreign-indigenous debate, with members of parliament insisting that more needs to be done to ensure that Ugandans, notably Africans, get a "fair" share of the assets on sale. The indigenous argument comes at a time when the government has precious little means of directly assisting Africans, other than via better information. The second set of questions, closely related to the first, regards control. As Uganda's parastatal experience has shown, ownership can be a far remove from actual control. To reach the goals of privatisation: increased efficiency, higher employment and growth, the privatised companies need to be restructured and re-capitalised. The latter demand in turn that there be real owners i.e. those that can exercise control via acquisition of adequate capital as well as management skills. Ironically, emphasising "control" works against local (indigenous) bids because they often lack capital and management skills.

However, it has been argued that since privatisation is only the beginning of a process of market development, indigenous firms should be assisted. It is only by participating at an early stage that local entrepreneurs will be able to acquire the "learning by doing skills" needed to ensure their participation in the future.

The third question relates to the twin issues of corporate governance and market development. While it is tempting to think of privatisation as an event, it is more appropriate to think of it as a complex of events whose outcome is linked to the policy environment, including legislation. Furthermore, the country needs to evolve a market culture, including corporate governance that is consistent with an expanding and increasingly complex economy. Ultimately, the operation of the stock exchange, the extent of tax compliance and fiscal rectitude depend on the success achieved in developing this culture.

There are, however, a number of more specific ways in which privatisation can be beneficial to the operation of the economy. It increases the incentive of owners to monitor managers. It is, however, debatable whether the goal of privatisation should be to ensure as broad an ownership pattern for each individual firm as possible or whether to ensure that privatised firms have "real" owners. Widespread share ownership creates a powerful lobby for the private sector and becomes a guarantee against re-nationalisation. Gray (1996) has argued, however, that in light of the major restructuring and management problems facing newly privatised companies, it is necessary to make sure that the new owners have the power and incentive to monitor the activities of their managers. The case for privatisation could also be based on the need for governments to establish reputation. In undertaking privatisation, governments signal to potential investors the course of future policies. It thus ties the hands of future governments, with policy makers wary of undertaking policies that have adverse impacts on the private sector. More predictable policies improve the planning horizon of economic agents, reducing the risks related to investment. However, while policy signalling is important for all countries, it has been even more crucial for those where nationalisation formed the thrust of economic policy in earlier years and where unsuccessful reform inflicted serious damage to the credibility of governments. In this respect, privatisation marks a break with the past: the market becomes an agent of restraint, while the risk of bankruptcy enforces discipline. Subjecting firms to market discipline is thus the single most important outcome of privatisation.

Privatisation in Uganda has been undertaken under the Public Enterprise Restructuring and Development (PERD) Statute No.9, 1993. The Statute (and subsequent amendments) divided the parastatals into groups: those in which the State would have 100 per cent ownership; those in which the State would require majority shareholding; enterprises to be fully divested; and enterprises to be liquidated. However, a revision of the Statute in 1997, led to an increase in the number of parastatals slated for outright privatisation and a reduction in those to be preserved in government control. While divestitures accumulated rapidly in the first three years after the introduction of the PERD statute, the pace slowed down as the larger and more demanding companies came on stream.

By December 1997, Uganda had privatised 78 public enterprises, accounting for over 77 per cent of the total of 102 companies targeted for privatisation by the Statute (and its amendments). About 20 companies had been struck off the company register while 12 remained in State hands.

The practical aspects of privatisation have been more demanding than anticipated. First was the need to create the infrastructure necessary for the exercise. In Uganda's case the Statute established a Divestiture and Reform Implementation Committee, whose directives would be carried out by the Enterprise Development, with two units: 1. The Parastatal Monitoring Unit and 2. The Privatisation Unit. At the apex, the privatisation effort is led by a Minister of State for Finance (Privatisation). Furthermore, privatisation could not have gone ahead without special legislation. Thus to allow other participants in the electricity sector a strategic plan had to be developed for it as well as a new Electricity Act to replace the old one from the 1960s which had conferred a monopoly for power generation on the Uganda Electricity Board. Likewise to enable entry of other participants in the telecommunications sector new legislation was needed, hence the recently passed Communications Bill. A new telecommunications company, MNTel has entered the Uganda market as the second telecommunications operator.

Besides legislation, government also tried to popularise privatisation via public education exercises, including radio shows, meetings and discussions with leaders of opinion (such as members of parliament) where the benefits of privatisation are highlighted.

However, although by the end of the 1990s, Uganda's privatisation exercise had gone so far that it could not be reversed at small cost, the subject remains controversial and members of parliament feel that some aspects of it need to be revisited. Of much concern is how the money received is being spent and why there has been such little transparency in the activities of the Privatisation Unit. The privatisation scandals in Uganda, brewing for most of the second half of 1998, reached a head with the resignation of two key members of the government directly responsible for privatisation.

In terms of fiscal impact, the effects of privatisation on public finances have mostly been indirect. For example, although the government had privatised assets worth US$100 million by 1995, only 40 per cent had been paid in cash, while substantial amounts went towards settling corporate debts and paying off workers. However, a "subsidy study" revealed that the government still provided over US$200 million in subsidies to the parastatals that remained in government hands. This could be compared to the US$500 million that the country collected in taxes in 1995. Thus the biggest benefit to government of privatisation will be the sharp reduction in its subsidies to the business sector, and later the contribution that the expanded private sector will be making in terms of providing a broader tax base.

In terms of output, if not employment, privatisation has had a strong impact. Companies such as Hima Cement, privatised at the end of 1995, increased production from virtually nothing to 600 metric tonnes of cement per day. The number of employees doubled to 800. The soft drinks and beverages sector has seen the most dramatic turnaround. They now produce enough to meet the country's needs and are looking for export possibilities. In contrast, firms still in the public sector have continued to perform badly. The Uganda Railways, for example, has recently had to abandon its western route and to curtail services on others in a bid to save money.

IV.1.3. The private/public sector boundary

Creation of an enabling environment

Irrespective of the privatisation modalities, the "new" industries will not grow nor prosper in a vacuum. The size and assets of the privatised firms are often poor indicators of future performance, since they were acquired under a different market regime. Part of the government's responsibility is to create the conditions under which the "new" firms can thrive after privatisation. This necessitates the removal of constraints to the business environment in areas such as taxation, property ownership, credit access, and laws related to bankruptcy. To improve the competitiveness of the privatised firms, cost-saving, quality-improving and energy-saving investments need to be undertaken. These have to be financed, which is another important factor to address. Measures that improve credit availability have a direct and positive impact on the success of privatisation. Finally, firm performance is also dependent on the availability of a functioning economic and social infrastructure.

Corruption and rent-seeking activities have been impediments to investment in Uganda. As has been well explored in the literature (Wade, 1985), corrupt activities demand real resources, not least in time and money, while they add little or nothing to total output. How can government deal with corruption without taking the economy back to the controls of the past? Market reforms such as those related to foreign exchange transactions have eliminated a number of discrepancies. But the culture of transparency takes time to build. In fact when public sector reforms imply costs or loss of incomes to influential groups they will be resisted (Schiavo-Campo, 1996; Robinson, 1990). The opposition to the introduction of value added tax (VAT) in many African countries is illustrative. Since VAT is incurred by the final consumer, it is thus less distortionary than other taxes. Nevertheless in many countries its loudest opponents have been urban producers and traders. One of the reasons for this has been that administration of the tax demands the keeping of records, which in turn increases tax liability. The latter might fall more heavily on the poorer end of the businesses than on the bigger and more influential ones.

To improve incentives in central government, many African countries have instituted specialised agencies for the performance of key tasks, such as tax collection, investment promotion and the undertaking of key projects in line ministries. Revenue authorities have been set up in many countries including Uganda, Tanzania, Ghana and Zambia, with support from the international financial institutions. These have in many cases been accompanied by one-stop investment agencies. Common for these institutions are the much better wages for their workers than for comparable work in the civil service. These new initiatives have had dramatic impacts on tax collection and on the mobilisation of domestic and foreign investment. However, the exposure of a relatively small group of employees to a large and expanding private sector, has taken its toll. There are reports of forgeries, bribery and collapsing morale. In the Uganda Revenue Authority, one of the first ones in the region, mass layoffs are frequently used to "unclog" the system.

While the pace of privatisation has been rapid in some countries, manufacturing output growth has remained weak. The change of ownership has not removed the structural weaknesses of the former parastatals. Before privatisation, parastatals enjoyed credits and subsidies from government, but since private alternatives are still inadequate, and with equity markets too small to cater for the needs of the embryonic private sector, privatised companies still have poor access to capital. They have not been able to rehabilitate equipment or introduce new technologies. Governments have also been slow in instituting the appropriate legal framework to support the private sector, including transfer and protection of property rights. On the other hand, the skill composition of the labour force was earlier disproportionately geared towards public sector work and privatised enterprises now lack an adequate supply of managers, technicians and planners to operate firms in the changed market situation.

With regard to investment incentives, the government has removed all non-neutral measures, such as tax holidays for foreign investors, which have tended to favour speculative investment. A new tax code, which incorporates all the incentives for both domestic and foreign investors, was presented to parliament. The new code will address the private sector's demands for a simpler tax administration; expand the tax base (and thereby reduce the tax burden on individual businesses).

Still, without the supportive role of fully developed financial sectors, efficient markets will not be able to develop in Uganda. Thus the reform of the financial sector is one of the most important interventions to be undertaken. The banking sector still suffers from the hangover of a bad loan portfolio accumulated in the 1970s and 1980s. For example, the Uganda Commercial Bank lent huge amounts to politicians from successive regimes, and had huge non-performing assets by the late 1980s. In preparing for privatisation, there was retrenchment of employees, as well as branch closures. The non-performing assets of the bank were also placed in a "bad" bank, and properties of the debtors auctioned. At the end of 1997, 49 per cent of the shares of the Uganda Commercial Bank were sold to Westmont Land (Asia) Bhd of Malaysia. A year later, however, the deal was suspended by the Ministry of Finance and Economic Planning owing to the serious anomalies that had crept into the management of the institution since the deal was struck. Westmont Land was used as a front by powerful domestic groups to obtain cheap credit, thus contravening the letter (and the spirit) of the take-over agreement.

Constraints on firm activities

In this section we look at a number of institutional constraints that affect the performance of the private sector in Uganda, using data from a survey of private firms undertaken at the end of 1994 that covered most parts of the country. The results are presented in Tables IV.1 and IV.2 by size and sector of affiliation, respectively. Firms were asked to indicate, on a scale of 1, for no problem, to 5, for serious problem, how serious a particular institutional constraint was on their operation. Table IV.1 shows that, irrespective of the size of the firm taxes and the cost of finance were found to be serious operational constraints. As already discussed above, the government's limited tax base and poor capacity for collection of taxes in the informal sector has meant an unusually large burden on firms. Likewise, poor financial intermediation and the effects of a bad loan portfolio from the past have meant that interest rates have remained high, even as inflation has fallen in the past decade. Taken as a whole, poor infrastructure provision is also a serious impediment to operation.

Table IV.1. *Medium-term constraints on firms by firm size, 1994* (*average scores: 1=no obstacle, 5=severe obstacle*)

	Micro (1-5) n=46	Small (6-20) n=86	Medium (21-50) n=72	Large (50-100) n=26	Very large (over 100) n=35	Average score
Taxes	3.67	3.83	3.79	3.56	3.86	3.74
Cost of finance	2.97	3.44	3.65	3.72	3.42	3.44
Infrastructure	3.06	2.81	3.14	3.36	3.17	3.1
Demand conditions	1.95	2.58	2.61	3.0	3.22	2.7
Economic policy uncertainty	2.45	2.56	2.57	2.76	2.68	2.6
Procurement of inputs	2.15	2.56	2.57	2.5	2.37	2.43
Labour market	1.67	2.09	2.33	2.6	2.62	2.22
Business support services	1.91	2.17	2.21	2.56	2.26	2.22
Trade regulations	1.65	2.09	2.1	2.32	2.7	2.17

Source: World Bank: Uganda Private Enterprise Survey, 1994.

Demand conditions are most constraining for the bigger companies i.e. those with more than 50 employees. Although at 20 million the Ugandan market is potentially large, low incomes imply a very low purchasing power. The big firms are thus demand constrained and have to work under available capacities. The smaller firms, on the other hand, seem less burdened by market demand. They are in most cases into consumer, notably food, products and thus have a ready domestic market. However, the manufacturing sector needs to be able to export to regional markets and further afield. This is the best way to improve standards and to find competitive niches in the global economy. The other constraints were fairly mild: economic policy uncertainty, procurement of inputs, the labour markets, business support services or trade regulations. The latter indicates that a fair amount of market liberalisation has taken place, although the bigger firms are still more constrained by the business environment than smaller ones. It is probably worth noting that the labour market in Uganda has been "free" for a long time. The sharp decline of employment opportunities in the past decimated the labour union's power. Employers set wages pretty much as they like.

In Table IV.2 we present the results by industry of affiliation. Taxes and the cost of finance are again shown to be serious constraints. Taxes are especially serious for the commerce sector and agro-industry. These two sectors provide the bulk of consumer goods and were seriously affected by the government's tightening of tax collection. Most firms state that it is not so much the taxes that are the problem but the fact that taxes are paid without a visible improvement in service provision, and hence no reduction in their transaction costs. Infrastructure constraints are shown to be most serious for industry and services but are lower for the other sectors. Demand conditions, though less serious, are significant for industry and construction. It is noteworthy that industry (non-food related) suffers from procurement problems, probably related in turn to poor transport, since the bulk of inputs is imported. For agro-industry, however, much of the input is from domestic sources.

Table IV.2. *Medium-term constraints on firms by sector, 1994*
(average scores: 1=no obstacle, 5=severe obstacle)

	Industry n=75	Agro-industry n=34	Commerce n=53	Services n=76	Construction n=27	Average score
Taxes	3.68	3.81	4.05	3.75	3.46	3.74
Cost of finance	3.46	3.87	3.36	3.21	3.65	3.65
Infrastructure	3.45	2.96	2.66	3.04	2.77	3.1
Demand conditions	2.86	2.45	2.30	2.54	2.84	2.7
Economic policy uncertainty	2.57	2.75	2.67	2.44	2.61	2.6
Procurement of inputs	3.36	2.66	2.16	2.29	2.34	2.43
Labour market	2.52	2.0	1.73	2.14	2.65	2.22
Business support services	2.09	2.48	2.26	2.09	2.19	2.22
Trade regulations	2.32	2.03	2.6	1.62	2.2	2.17

Source: World Bank: Uganda Private Enterprise Survey, 1994.

Based on information from 1994, the two tables are a "mid-term" assessment of Uganda's business environment. They indicate that a number of lingering constraints remain. There was a general feeling among firms that the tax burden was too high, while the provision of infrastructure services was poor. Moreover, the cost of finance was raising the costs of production and depressing demand. To resolve these problems, the government has sought to deepen financial sector reforms and to undertake a more rapid rehabilitation and extension of the infrastructure.

Weak institutions and privatisation

In a recent article, the *New Vision* (16 December 1998) presented parts of the *Report of the Parliament's Select Committee on Privatisation*. The report argues that political interference has undermined the privatisation process. A number of anomalies were highlighted: for instance, while the law requires that the Privatisation Unit keep payments from sales of public enterprises in interest bearing accounts, pending the conclusion of the sale agreement, this generally has not been the case. Moreover, the stipulation that successful purchases pay not less than 50% of the full purchase price on settlement, with the balance payable over a period not exceeding twelve months, has also been violated.

A sample of privatised firms showed that owing to lack of transparency at the Privatisation Unit many of the stipulations were ignored. Moreover, there was "a lot of influence peddling". The slow privatisation of companies like Uganda Airlines, Coffee Marketing Board, Air Cargo etc can partly be blamed on this. Political influence has also affected the tendering process and final settlement as in the case of Uganda Grain Milling, ENHAS (the cargo handling company at Entebbe Airport), Uganda Commercial Bank, etc. The Committee also felt that, under pressure from influential groups, the Privatisation Unit, failed to consider other privatisation options, for example sale to employees or members of the public via the newly established stock exchange. Moreover, there were cases of asset stripping or where monopolies were left intact after privatisation.

Some of the problems encountered were a result of the loopholes in the PERD Statute (i.e. the privatisation law). The law for example provides that the liabilities of the privatised companies be deducted from the divestiture account (i.e. all the accumulated sales) apparently without limit. Managers thus tended to accumulate debts and other liabilities pre-privatisation in the hope that these would be settled from the divestiture account. Considerable expenses also went towards paying consultants' fees and merchant banks for evaluation services, apparently without regard to the possible sales value of the company. The divestiture account is thus virtually empty today.

During the Consultative Group (CG) meeting in Kampala in December 1998, the donor community was very supportive of the work of the Parliamentary Committee. They saw it as good for keeping privatisation on track for the benefit of the country, rather than merely politically well connected people.

Recently, the government (Inspector General of Government—IGG) commissioned a national integrity survey which looked, among other things at the level of corruption in government, especially the instances providing basic services and those responsible for the enforcement of law and order. Indicating the extent of corruption, the police and the judiciary top the list of the most corrupt institutions in the country. In Table III.4 we use information from the Integrity Report to relate the percentages of respondents reporting that they paid a bribe for a service, with those reporting satisfaction with delivery.

Table IV.3. *Payment of bribes and satisfaction with service, 1998*
(% of respondents, mean bribe in shillings in brackets)

Institution/service	Payment of bribes		Satisfaction with service (%)
Health	28	(12,000)	63
Local government	39	(50,450)	53
URA (Taxes)	40	(15,300)	46
Judiciary	50	(106,500)	36
Police	63	(72,000)	36

Note: 1 US$=1,150 shillings (average 1998).
Source: IGG/CIET International: Uganda National Integration Survey, 1998.

The Table shows that of the 28 per cent of the respondents seeking health care paid a bribe of about 12,000 shillings, with a median of 3,500. The latter is interesting because it implies that 50 per cent of those paying bribes to health workers paid less than this amount, that is less than $3 per visit. This is not excessive. The amounts could be seen as "topping-up" strategies (and also that the poor are over represented among those seeking public health care and can only afford a small bribe). The figures change radically when it comes to the judiciary. Here, an average bribe is close to 110,000 shillings with the median at 50,000. It is difficult to see this as a "topping-up" or even a strategy for expediting justice.

Still, it is interesting to note that on the whole the size of the bribing activity (here given as the percentage of respondents giving a bribe for a service) does not seem to improve service delivery. Thus although only 28 per cent of respondents seeking healthcare report paying a bribe to health workers, 65 per cent are satisfied with the speed at which the service is provided. Surprisingly, only 36 per cent of the respondents in the case of the police and the judiciary, respectively, are satisfied with the speed of service delivery, even though a large percentage of respondents paid a bribe.[9] Barring the difficulties of weighting the various incidences of corruption and their seriousness, it must be encouraging to note that for society as a whole corruption is a mere waste of resources.

Corruption in education was found to be low in the Integrity Survey. Since Uganda schools have continued to perform well in regional comparison this should not be surprising. Here competition between institutions, both private and public, and a reasonable level of regulation by the government has ensured the maintenance of standards. But, an important factor in the education sector has been the active participation of the population at large via the Teacher and Parents' Associations, for example. This has heightened the level of transparency, a crucial ingredient in the fight against corruption.

---

9. Of course, causality could run the other way, but this does not seem to be the case.

Corruption and market liberalisation

Since corruption exists in one form or another in most countries, it would seem that the inter-country differences in its spread and level are determined by what each individual society (via the dictates of its social/cultural norms, legal systems and resources directed at fighting it) tolerates or finds "comfortable" to live with—and this might of course vary greatly from country to country. Thus, put simply, the recent anti-corruption outcry in Uganda indicates that the population (or more accurately the opinion makers) find the current level of corruption in the country to have exceeded the "accepted" or "normal" level.

This suggests two possible conclusions. First, one could argue, as indeed has been done in recent months, that corruption in Uganda has risen in both relative (for example compared to earlier regimes or neighbouring countries) and absolute terms (for example, that there have been increases in the total number of corruption episodes or volume of cash and assets involved). Second, a case could be made that following a decade of steady economic improvement, increase in some civil liberties and a more market-oriented management of the economy (not to forget the emergence of a more vocal press) the population's tolerance of corruption has declined. This is of course the same as saying that the demands of the public with respect to the rectitude of holders of public office have been raised. That the public is more willing than before to oppose corruption. Thus ironically, the present outcry might be more a reflection of the success of the reforms ushered in by the government, especially those aspects which have helped evolve an "anti-corruption mood" among the population, than an escalation of corruption *per se*. If this conclusion is right then we could say that the dynamics of a market economy have caused a transition of corruption tolerance.

In a market environment, actors enjoy a better flow of information, regarding market opportunities, and prices etc. Corruption can thus be seen as an attempt by some individuals to circumvent the information flow and to create "corruption rents", which, to be meaningful (or worth the risk) have to be enjoyed by exclusive groups. If allowed to expand, this would end up recreating the control regime of the past. However, private actors enter the market because they want to share in the profit generating process and will not tolerate for long individuals or groups that block information flows or that attempt to "pick winners". Thus to some extent, the corruption debate in Uganda also depicts struggles within the private sector for the right to play on a level field. That the debate is going on is a positive indicator that the market economy is taking root.

IV.1.4. Conclusions

This section has looked at the public sector's changing role in Uganda and the emergence of a competitive private sector. The transformation has been two-fold: first, there has been a change in structure, with public enterprises sold outright or put under private management. Second, there has been a radical change in policy emphasis with controls giving way to market promotion and private sector development. The transition from economies dominated by public enterprises to those functioning under private competition has been complicated by structural constraints, including poorly developed credit markets, inadequate economic infrastructure and even political opposition. But perhaps the most serious impediment to reform has been the public sector itself. Even after the retrenchment of the civil service, it has been difficult to considerably improve conditions in the public sector owing to slow learning and system failures.[10]

There has been a growing perception in recent years, that corruption is widespread in the country. The system to sanction corruption is still very inefficient and the cases reported are not dealt with rapidly or effectively. Uganda is thus ranked low in an international comparison based on interviews with private firms.[11] However, the situation seems somewhat less endemic or systemic than in some neighbouring countries. There, individuals acquire positions with the understanding that they will use them to reap as much "rent" as possible. Public office is thus a form of reward for political loyalty.

IV.2 Good governance and policy reform: Prospects and obstacles

IV.2.1 Introduction

Though Uganda's civil service was renowned for its efficiency in the 1960s, it was more or less decimated in the 1970s under the rule of Idi Amin. Governments that followed were unable to stabilise the economy. Public sector wages became irrelevant, and employees stayed on for other reasons, including the possibility of "privatising" parts of the public service, such as official stamps and licences. On assuming power in 1986, the National Resistance Movement (NRM) tried to improve discipline and raise effort in the public sector, by initially appealing to the loyalty, even patriotism, of the civil servants. It was noted that while "casualisation" of the public services was an important survival mechanism for civil servants during the period of chaos, enabling workers to engage in supplementary income-generating activities outside government, recovery demanded an efficient public sector. Experience has shown

---

10. A survey (CIET international, 1998) of the integrity of the law implementing and regulatory agencies in Uganda, such as the police, judicial organs, and local administration, found a considerable amount of corruption. A substantial share of recent revelations of malpractice are related to military procurement and contract.

11. In a recent report by Langseth, Pezullo, and Simpkin (1998), which was presented at a meeting of Transparency International in Malaysia is noted: The political will of high (Ugandan) government officials to fight corruption is wanting. It is generally believed by stakeholders that, while President Museveni is capable of curbing the high level of Grand Corruption evident in Uganda, he has become evidently less willing to do so. Statements by the President which demonstrate this shift in outlook include "corruption is not hurting development as long as the money does not leave Uganda", "Money laundering is good for Uganda as long as the money is not leaving the country".

that much more needed to be done to create the kind of public sector that would be responsive to the needs of the private sector and the rest of the economy.

IV.2.2. Public sector reform

Following preparatory plans involving interviews with over 25,000 civil servants and political leaders during 1989–90, the Public Service Review and Re-Organisation Commission presented a White Paper on Public Service Reform in 1991. Already by 1992 some 4,000 workers "drunkards and non-performers" as described in the newspapers had been dismissed. However, this figure fell far short of that expected by donors. Still the government felt politically constrained from too rapid a retrenchment. Four years later, by 1996, the government had successfully removed close to 150,000 employees from public service.

Civil or public service reform had two main objectives: first, payment of at least a "living wage" to its employees, and second, introduction of a results oriented management style to ensure better public service delivery. In application, there was need for rationalisation of the work of the central ministries and the districts, the goal being to have a smaller and more accountable organisation that focused on core services, leaving the non-core to the private sector. The Re-Organisation Commission recommended a 50 per cent reduction of public sector employees as well as a sharp increase in remuneration. The retrenchment was effected partly by discharging workers that had reached retirement age, ridding the system of "ghost workers" i.e. workers not physically identifiable (although on the payroll). Other measures included voluntary retirements and freezing of civil service recruitment (in 1990), and creation of a Payroll Monitoring Unit in the Ministry of Public Service.

The retrenchment was followed by monetisation of allowances and benefits such as housing, food allowances etc.[12] with a view to raising transparency and removing distortions. As a per cent of non-debt recurrent expenditure, the public sector wage bill increased from 21 per cent in fiscal 1993/94 to 40 per cent in 1997/98. In terms of GDP, the wage rose over this short period from 1.8 to 3.6 per cent. To increase incentives at the administrative level, public sector emoluments have risen by a considerable amount. In dollar terms the monthly wage of a permanent secretary rose from about 36 in 1993 to 1,550 in 1997. At the lower levels wages have risen as well though not as dramatically.

To ensure that the reforms in the public service are permanent, the implementing agency (Ministry of Public Service) needed to be strengthened, especially in terms of management capacity. There was need for job coding and the assurance that individuals could once again make a career in the civil

---

12. Uganda had before the reform over 60 wage categories accompanied by 70 different types of allowances and benefits.

service. A code of conduct and discipline was also necessary to uphold standards and to help develop a new work culture. Among the achievements of the reform has been the perceptible increase in morale in the public service and the increase in service delivery. Above all, the reform has been undertaken without the rancour that has characterised public sector reforms in other countries.

Instrumental to the success of the reforms was the unadulterated support of the leaders. There was broad agreement on the problems to be resolved. The leadership saw the restoration of integrity and accountability that would result as crucial to its political agenda. This commitment made it possible to reach a set of feasible programmes and to commit budgetary resources. However, support from donors, who were impressed by the government's plans was important for the success of the programme. Thus while the government spent up to US$30 million on the programme between 1993–95, donors pledged some US$20 million for compensation of the retrenched. It is also said that reforms succeeded because there were still a few people in the system who still remembered what an efficient civil service was like, they helped recreate and internalise a vision of the new Ugandan public service.

With regard to the future, the Minister of Public Service (Uganda, 1997a) has noted in an introduction to a programme statement for 1997–2002 that "We must build a public service which is capable of meeting the demands of an expanding and increasingly complex economy". Among the immediate challenges is how to enlarge local capacities for management and policy formulation at the centre and in the districts. A considerable amount of work in the public service reform area has been undertaken with assistance from expatriate staff, with local personnel taking over more and more of the responsibilities. Related to this will be the creation of systems that limit corruption and enhance integrity. With regard to the latter, the new Parliament is taking a tough stance against corruption, while the office of the Inspector General of Government is more active.[13]

The government, with assistance from the World Bank has already embarked on extensive capacity building, especially at the local levels where future development interventions will take place. There has been a special focus on financial and personnel management, especially public accounts, as well as creation of incentives for employees at the various levels to excel. The goal is to increase the efficiency of resource use. The legal departments have been weak in the past and also are targeted for support. In building local capacities, attempts will be made to put together a monitoring scheme that is able to trace improvements or where changes need to be made. Still, institutional outcomes can be disappointing and one needs to be clear about the focus that their activities will have in order to ensure effectiveness.

---

13. A junior minister was recently censored by parliament for corruption.

Finally, for the programmes to be sustainable, the government needs to create a synergetic relationship with the private sector. "The private sector will view the public service as a partner and facilitator, not as a bureaucratic hindrance" (Uganda, 1997a, d). This will imply that many of the services supplied by the government today will probably be taken over by the private sector in the future. But it also means that the public sector needs to develop a system that provides adequate information on business generated by government tenders. To ensure fairness, the government has established a tax tribunal, as well as a commercial court to adjudicate business disagreements expeditiously.

IV.2.3. Decentralisation

Decentralisation was a lead theme of Museveni's National Resistance Movement from the "bush days" of the early 1980s. Museveni (1997) has argued that the emphasis on problem resolution by broad consensus, while cumbersome, proved to be the glue that held his movement and army together in the early, and difficult, phase of the struggle. This early experience was to become the blueprint for the broader decentralisation effort. Kisakye (1996) has argued that resistance councils were conceived as vehicles for self-determination and self-governance. They would be the instruments that would restore democracy, help involve the population in the process of national development, bring about social justice and mobilise the people in production (see also Collins and Green, 1994). Above all the RCs were seen as channels for the consolidation of power of the National Resistance Movement, a point on which there has been criticism from the Movement's political opponents in Uganda and abroad.

In practice decentralisation has proven to be a more extensive and complex exercise that what the government could have imagined. It started with the abrogation of the Local Administrations Act of 1969 and the institution, a bare seven months after taking power, of a commission of inquiry into local government.[14] By the end of the 1990s, the decentralisation effort had clearly transcended any earlier ambitions at political mobilisation (Uganda, 1997a, b).

In an evaluation, Langseth (1996) has named the following as the main objective of decentralisation in Uganda: a move towards more democratic government that is responsible and accountable to the public. It would promote capacity building at the local level and ensure that there are local inputs in the decision-making process, especially with regard to delivery of services. Above all, decentralisation would help foster local "ownership" of development programmes. The goals of decentralisation have had broad support from donors (see also Langseth and Mugaju, 1996; Uganda, 1997d).

---

14. Mahmood Mamdani, an outstanding Ugandan academic who was very active in the reform debate in the 1980s, chaired the commission.

However, real and potential difficulties facing the new structures should not be underestimated. Uganda has a serious shortage of resources and skills: physical facilities are inadequate and the general infrastructure in the rural areas is not conducive to rapid development. Policy impulses are supposed to emanate from the central ministries, but these have been undergoing rapid changes themselves (Villadsen and Lubanga, 1996).

Political decentralisation had to evolve in tandem with financial decentralisation. Budgetary and spending powers had to be devolved to the districts. The Local Government Commission was established in 1993, with its provisions enshrined in the Uganda Constitution of 1995. The goal of financial decentralisation was to assign responsibilities and taxes between the centre and local governments, as well as to enable transfer of grants and other resources. The first item on the agenda was to decentralise the central budget. How was this to be done in a country up to now steered from the centre? A block grant system was devised, where central government would allocate funds to the districts based on the level of programmes of the line ministries in each district. This was seriously flawed and was replaced by an allocation system based on a "needs based formula" with a weighting of 10 per cent for the area, 10 for the size of the general population, 40 per cent for the school-age population and 40 per cent for child mortality.[15] But since this weighting does not take into account the capacities to collect taxes in the various districts a degree of inequitable resource distribution remains. Other problems were that unconditional grants were based on rather poor wage calculations so that attracting officers from the centre proved difficult.

There was a phased financial decentralisation. It began with budgetary votes to 13 districts in the 1993/94 financial year, followed by 14 in the 1994/95 financial year, while votes were introduced for the last set of districts in 1995/96. In the year following the introduction of budgetary votes, districts then reverted to block grants.

Two other grants are the conditional grant, first introduced in 1996/97, and the equalising grant, not yet provided for in the budget. Conditional grants, as their name suggests, were to be based on certain conditions. However, although the conditional grants for 1996/97 were disbursed, related conditionalities are not yet defined. The Local Government Finance Commission suggests that conditional grants could be a mixture of demand-driven initiatives to get districts to undertake projects in, say, poverty reduction, that they otherwise would not have done. In each case, central and district authorities would agree on the level of conditionality and how to enforce it. The grant equalisation grant will be based on an assessment of resource endowments: an exercise bound to be controversial.

The success of decentralisation will depend on the capacity of the districts and urban governments to raise their own revenue and use it efficiently in the

---

15. Child mortality refers to those aged 0–59 months.

provision of services. In rural Uganda the Graduated Personal Tax (GPT) has been in operation for a long time. It is relatively simple and accepted by the majority of the people. The Local Finance Commission (1997) suggests that to boost local tax collection and encourage self-sufficiency, the tax effort should be related to the conditional grants from the centre.

For decentralisation to succeed, there has to be a high level of public accountability. In this regard, the Local Government Finance Commission has registered a number of accountability problems in the districts. Budgetary discipline is weak. In some cases, there is a total lack of budgetary procedures or trained staff to do the work. Furthermore, there is lack of transparency in the use of funds, especially in the award of tenders for the supply of goods and services. Records are generally poorly audited, while in many cases not at all. Although Rakai District managed to achieve a rapid improvement in service provision, thanks to donor assistance (Semakula, 1996), governance issues and corruption reversed some of the progress.

IV.2.4. Conclusion

One important ingredient of public sector reform is the creation of a professional and well-run civil service. During the crisis years the real incomes of the civil service in Uganda had declined dramatically, and the morale and effectiveness of the service was very low. The NRM government has managed to retrench surplus staff, and to increase salaries to more decent levels.

The decentralisation process is a real challenge for the government. It is essentially a good strategy for the long term development of the regions outside the capital, but there is a glaring gap between the plans and the actual capacity and competence on the ground. Since the decentralised councils are to handle important services such as health and education it is essential that these be strengthened.

Part V
Discussion and conclusion

V.1. Introduction

The starting point for this project was the proposition that to maximise impact donors should seek out successful African countries and concentrate aid to those. The argument is that these would then become leaders for the rest. We presented a set of criteria to help us investigate whether Uganda is such an economy and whether it can be said to have taken off into self-sustaining growth. In this section we discuss these issues in light of the evidence, and reach some conclusions.

V.2. Is Uganda an emerging economy?

During the last decade Uganda has managed to maintain an impressive annual growth rate of 6.4 per cent or 3.3 per cent in per capita terms. Initially during the reform period, growth was achieved mainly via improvements in the policy environment and by the (partial) restoration of peace, making it possible to rehabilitate facilities and increase capacity utilisation. In the longer term, however, growth also requires an increase in the factors of production, particularly capital, and technological progress. Both require investment. In the past few years, private investment has increased, much of it by domestic investors, but with a substantial inflow of foreign investment. Growth in the latter part of the reform period has to a high degree been based on investments in new capacity. As noted above, the war in the Congo and other regional conflicts might slow down this expansion. Investors perceive the risk to be substantial and are therefore cautious.

Let us now review Uganda's performance according to the criteria presented in the introductory chapter.

A: Macroeconomic aspects

1) Macroeconomic stability. Sound fiscal and monetary policies are prerequisites for successful development, and the stabilisation efforts in Uganda have, in this respect, after some initial setbacks, been successful. The Ministry of Finance is keeping tight controls on spending and is committed to the preservation of stability. It collaborates closely with the Bank of Uganda, which in recent years has helped to sustain a fairly responsible monetary policy. Inflation is under control. However, much of the persistence of the stabilisation efforts is due to the commitment of a small circle of individuals in the Ministry of Finance and Economic Planning. Still, the staff in the ministry has by now been actively involved in policy making over a number of years and has acquired a good understanding of the issues involved.

Sufficient revenue collection is a basic requirement for self-sustaining growth. If this is not achieved, the government would have to continue to rely on foreign aid for financing. If part of the aid inflow is used to help reduce the tax burden on the private sector and thus facilitate its expansion, then aid dependency need not be a threat. The Uganda Revenue Authority has not been able to build on its initial success, and, from a low base, revenue collection has stagnated around 11–12 per cent of GDP. The problem now is not so much lack of statutes or regulations but rather their proper implementation in order to remove institutional inefficiencies and the administrative problems related to revenue collection. There are often no proper accounts in firms, creating scope for personal discretion and corruption.

2) International competitiveness. One important indicator of whether Uganda has taken off is whether it has become internationally competitive in areas outside traditional commodity exports. There have been some breakthroughs, for example in horticulture. However, there are only a few manufacturing firms which have managed to profile themselves in regional trade. Uganda's external competitiveness is thus only improving slowly. Is it the case, as suggested by Wood (1994), that Africa does not have its comparative advantages in labour intensive manufacturing production, but rather that they are in production that uses intensively the abundant natural resources? One would in the Wood case expect improvements in land intensive exports. This is happening in the context of flower and fish exports, although in both cases "structural" impediments such as lack of refrigeration facilities at Entebbe or facilities for fish handling that meet EU specifications prevent rapid expansion. Still, results on African manufacturing exports reported in Bigsten et al. (1998) seem to suggest that there are important productivity effects of exporting. To be able to achieve rapid growth it is necessary to also make a breakthrough in the export of manufactures.

The process of trade liberalisation is well underway. There has been a shift towards tariffs from quantitative restrictions on imports, and those have been harmonised and lowered. Tariff revenues are, however, still an important revenue source for the government, which means that the pace of reform here will to some extent depend on the progress made with respect to tax revenue collection in the form of, for example, income taxes and VAT.

B: Microeconomic aspects

3) Competitive domestic markets. There is less government interference in domestic markets. One of the major gains for coffee producers in recent years, was the end of the Coffee Marketing Board's monopoly on the marketing of coffee. In many other areas competition is still weak, however. In the utilities, for example, the regulatory framework is yet to become operative.

4) A stable financial system. There has been some progress in efforts to create a more diversified and reliable financial system, but the sector is still fragile and prone to abuse. The weakness of the financial system, with few products, mostly confined to the capital, is a good illustration of the type of institutional constraints that the country still faces.

C: Human resources and infrastructure

5) Human capital for competitive production. Human capital development is crucial if growth is to be sustained. In the area of education there has been some progress with the introduction of UPE (with free education for at least four children per family). However, technical skills are scarce, with white-collar employment still the driving goal of education. However, countries that were able to industrialise also had a good supply of skilled labour. Uganda's healthcare services reach only a small portion of the population. The country has poorer health indicators than most African countries.

6) An effective physical infrastructure. Uganda has focussed on the development of the transportation network. The major trunk roads in the south are relatively good, while roads in northern Uganda remain poor. Energy and tele-communications are still major bottlenecks for large-scale producers. The restructuring of the telecommunications sector has, however, improved services while the electricity sector is similarly under restructuring.

D: Governance and politics

7) Unbiased institutions. Growth requires effective public institutions, such as courts, while the rule of law is essential for the development of a market economy. There have been some improvements and innovations in this area in Uganda, but the process is slow and inefficient. It has generally been difficult to bring cases to foreclosure. The independence of the private sector is increasing, however, although there is still undue interference from public sector agents. Notably, private banks have accumulated non-performing assets from politicians and their relatives.

8) Good governance. Growth requires good governance. The Ugandan public sector has been streamlined and there have been significant improvements in its effectiveness in the 1990s. Still, there is much rent seeking and corruption, with negative consequences for the economy. The decentralisation efforts undertaken in Uganda are interesting and will in the longer term probably make it easier to achieve development outside the core areas in the south of the country. However, local capacities are still low and funds are inefficiently used at the district level.

9) A broad-based development pattern. In terms of poverty reduction, there certainly has been progress, but in some regions, particularly those ravaged by guerrilla activity, the situation is desperate. This is a problem that cannot be solved by economic policy measures in a narrow sense. Still, to eliminate the basis for guerrilla opposition there is certainly a need for economic improvements in these regions. However, the problem is that while there is need for improvements, the instability there makes it hard to achieve.

10) Political maturity. The main constraints on Uganda's future growth are probably to be found in the political sphere. If there is too much corruption or political interference in economic activities escalates, the war in the Congo gets out of hand or if guerrillas now fighting government step up their activities, growth may come to a halt. This will lead to economic pressure and probably lead to policy reversal.

E: Self-reliance

11) Reduced aid dependence. The achievement of self-sustaining growth also requires that the country increasingly can grow from its own resources, that is a reduction of aid dependence. In the case of Uganda the aid inflows have remained unchanged in nominal terms in the last few years, but as the economy has grown quite rapidly there has also been a reduction in the extent of aid dependency, as measured by the aid/GDP ratio.

12) Controlled level of foreign debt. The debt reduction under the HIPC initiative has relieved the pressure on the budget. Donors still provide approximately the same amounts of aid as before, but the part that earlier went to debt servicing now can be used for domestic expenditures instead. So there is a double benefit for the country.

13) Domestic saving and foreign private investment as the major source of investment finance. A large share of investment is still financed by official foreign resources, but the domestic share has been increasing, while foreign private capital is flowing in as well.

On balance then, is Uganda on the path of self-sustaining economic growth? On the basis of the criteria we have laid down, the answer is no. The country has done well in the last decade, and has taken significant steps towards the creation of a market economy, but the growth momentum is still fragile. Aid dependency remains high, and it is not certain that positive per capita income growth can continue without aid. The political and institutional structures are weak and are an encumbrance to the effective functioning of the economy. There is still a lot of straddling by politicians or top level bureaucrats, making it difficult for the government to guarantee a level playing field in the private sector.

Yet, even if it is too early to say that Uganda has "taken off", it is definitely on the right track and further reform efforts deserve continued support. If the ambition of donors is to reward good effort, Uganda certainly is a good candidate.

V.3. Policy conclusions for Uganda

The main thrust of this study has been to investigate the extent to which the economic policies pursued by Uganda have contributed to growth. The results in Uganda, as summarised in the previous section, have been good on many fronts, and we will in this section discuss the major deficiencies that remain and what should be done to address them.

The introduction of a cash budget system helped to discipline the ministries and to maintain macroeconomic stability. However, a negative consequence of the system is increased volatility of expenditures. Eventually it should be possible to abandon the cash budget straightjacket. It is imperative, though, that this does not amount to the abandonment of control over the aggregate budget. Indeed with the current emphasis on decentralisation, budget procedures and transparency in implementation must be strengthened further. Much of the money that is allocated centrally never reaches the intended beneficiaries. To come to grips with this problem one has to have effective administrative systems and inculcate responsible behaviour. This is going to be very difficult as well as costly. Improving the level of remuneration of civil service is very important in this context.

Further improvements in taxation efforts are required. First, the efficiency and impartiality of tax collection must be enhanced. The government has made commendable attempts to do this by establishing a Commercial Court as well as a Tax Tribunal. Second, the tax base should be extended, while at the same time reducing the actual rates of taxation for some strategic types of incomes. Overall, the private sector firms need to be given some leeway to grow stronger before they can carry much taxation.

The emphasis is now on the development of the private sector within a market economy. Much needs to be done before private investors can feel that there is an enabling environment where investments are secure. For the time being investors are reluctant to invest long-term. The maintenance of macroeconomic stability is essential, but the focus now needs to be on the development of a fair system of taxation and a judicial system that can deal effectively with disputes.

Privatisation has gone a long way and should be continued until the targets set are reached. It is important, however, that transparency is improved and that fair bidding for property is allowed.

The preservation of a realistic exchange rate plus a continuation of the trade reform measures are necessary, but not sufficient, ingredients in a policy aimed at becoming competitive in the world market outside traditional areas.

Weak banks are a major problem. A whole range of measures are required to strengthen control of the financial system, which is misused by private agents as well as players in the public sector. The financial markets are very poorly developed, and the system needs to be reformed to make it possible for the Bank of Uganda to effectively pursue monetary policy via indirect monetary control. Still, the development of a stock market etc is a lower priority than to clean up the banking system.

By becoming the first HIPC programme beneficiary Uganda has managed to control the impact of its foreign debt well. This, therefore, does not seem to be a top priority any more, although the level of indebtedness is still high. It is important though, to sort out the arrears on domestic debt to support the creation of a functioning domestic credit market.

The poor delivery of public services in Uganda is a consequence of the virtual collapse of the public sector under Amin and in the subsequent turmoil, but there have been some improvements in the 1990s. However, most of the work remains to be done.

Ugandan growth has been mainly urban based, while at least the rural subsistence farmers have been left behind. Reintegration of these into the market economy will be essential for increasing their income. This reintegration of the rural population is being slowed down by the high petroleum tax. It will take time to reintegrate these groups, so in the short term the most effective way of increasing their standard of living may be via improved provision of social services.

There is a general concern that the poorest have not benefited much from the general improvements. Therefore efforts directed at reaching them need to continue. They have seen improved access to education, but direct private costs are still substantial enough to keep children of the poor out of school. Increased funding for education should be one of the top priorities of the government. Primary health care is another area which is very undersupplied with funds. In both these areas clients are forced to bribe their way through the system, and again there is a need to have a two-pronged strategy with administrative reforms and better salaries for employees.

V.4. What should donors do?

There exists a broad literature on the fungibility of aid.[16] Its main implication is that since aid is highly fungible donors should be concerned about the quality of the total expenditure programme of the recipient. This suggests in turn that donor co-ordination is important if the goal is to ensure that the allocation of resources reflects donor priorities.

---

16. Essentially, studies of fungibility have been time series country studies. The literature has produced mixed results, where there is fungibility in some instances but not in others. However, it has not dealt with Africa, so Devarajan, Rajkumar and Swaroop (1998) attempt to investigate this issue for Africa. They analyse a panel data set of 18 African countries. The analysis uses foreign aid variables, fiscal variables, and income and control variables. It looks at the allocation of aid across activities, but a limitation of the analysis is that they only have data on sector allocation with regard to loans and not with regard to grants. First, they show that there is no indication that governments reduce tax efforts when aid increases. An aid increase of one dollar increases government expenditure by 89 cents. About a third of the final increases goes to current expenditures, capital expenditures and principal repayment. The extent to which aid is fungible varies across sectors considered. Fungibility increases when monitoring is less efficient. This is measured by the number of donors involved in the sector in question assuming that more donors leads to less efficient monitoring. It is concluded that aid to agriculture, industry and health sectors is fully fungible, while loans to energy, transport and communications and education are only partially fungible.

One problem related to aid is that the mechanisms used to deliver it make administrators and politicians beholden to foreign constituencies rather than to their own. This leads to loss of accountability to domestic political process. Furthermore, the proliferation of externally-financed projects ties up recurrent outlays, and sometimes represents a large waste of time and managerial capabilities. Authority, control and accountability need to be returned to the recipient country government.[17]

One way of doing this is to reduce direct flows to the recipient country in the form of project and programme loans, but instead to use aid resources to reduce their debt burden. This will involve less direct interference in the affairs of the recipient country, at the same time as the resources released would have a beneficial effect. This, in essence, is the spirit of HIPC.

Alternatively, since NGOs operate more independently of the government, and do not withdraw as quickly from the country when policy disagreements arise, NGO funds are a less volatile and risky type of inflow from the recipient country's point of view. Moreover, aid through this channel does not affect the recipient government's activities to the same extent as official aid, and one could thus choose to deliver more aid via them. As this would not impose conditionality on the government, it would be free to work out its own policies. However, NGOs cannot substitute for an efficient public sector, but they may have a contribution to make in current efforts to reach the more disadvantaged segments of the population.

The creation of parallel structures for tax collection, investment promotion etc have worked fairly efficiently since they pay their employees well, but at the same time it leads to other problems in the general public service, where remuneration remains very low. This is further aggravated when donors, wishing to have their projects executed efficiently, offer special inducements to civil servants.

Uganda is one of the countries in Africa, which by now has a reasonably satisfactory policy environment, and it has been growing rapidly over the last decade. However, its investment rate remains fairly low, so the high growth is to a large extent the dividend of policy reform. Unless the investment rate can

---

17. One possible approach is developed by Kanbur (1998:4), who suggests the following: "Every year, the government would present its rolling three year (say) expenditure and revenue plan in the framework of an overall development strategy. These plans could be discussed with domestic and donor constituencies on the basis of which the donors would commit resources under certain broadly defined criteria, which do not go into minute details on individual projects. The plans would be scrutinised for broad coherence and feasibility, and policy consistency. But once this is done, donors would contribute to a pool of aid which, along with the government's own resources, would finance the entire expenditure package. There would be no sense in which each donor would require a detailed accounting for where its money went. The dialogue would focus on overall priorities and directions, and donors would not have the false comfort that their money is financing schools and not military expenditure. Most important of all, the time, energy and political capital of local officials would be saved for analysing and developing local priorities rather than managing the administration of a huge number of donor projects, each with its own accounting and administrative procedures. They would spend more time explaining the tradeoffs to their own people rather than negotiating with aid bureaucrats from donor agencies."

be raised the growth will not be sustainable in the longer term. Since domestic income levels are still low this will require external inflows of private and/or public investment resources. However, at present investors perceive risks to be high and many take a wait and see attitude. Recent studies have shown that aid can function as a catalyst for private investment (Burnside and Dollar, 1997) in a reformed policy environment, but there is also need for measures that either reduce risks or insure investors against risks if private investors are to come in on a large scale. Visible support from donors to countries that are on the right track would constitute a powerful signal to investors.

LIST OF PERSONS INTERVIEWED

Mr. Daniel S. Iga, Programme Officer, Danish Embassy, Kampala

Mr. Joseph S. Kitamirike, Manager, Regional Centres and Industrial Land Division, Uganda Investment Authority

Dr. Henry Opondo, Economist, Bank of Uganda

Mr. Jasper Aligawesa, Marketing Manager, Grand Imperial Hotel, Kampala

Mr. A.W. Walugembe-Musoke, Bank of Uganda

Mr. R. Rweikiza, Deputy Director of Research, Bank of Uganda

Mr. Damoni Kitabire, Director, Ministry of Finance

Mr. Yob Yobe Okello, Executive Director, Uganda Investment Authority

Mr. Karemente A. Kyoratungye, Head, Natural Resources, UIA

Ms. Elizabeth N. Ssemwanga, Head, Investment Facilitation, UIA

Ms. Mary E.S. Katarikawe, Economist, Bank of Uganda

Ms. Mary Muduuli, Director, Ministry of Finance and Economic Planning

Ms. Margaret Kakande, Poverty Analyst, Ministry of Finance and Economic Planning

Dr. J. Ddumba, Department of Economics, Makerere University

Dr. G. Ssemogerere, Department of Economics, Makerere University

Dr. A. Balihuta, Department of Economics, Makerere University

Mr. Wasswa Y. Kajubi, Executive Director, Private Sector Foundation

Mr. Patrick Banya, Director, Uganda Manufacturers Association

Mr. Japheth B. Katto, Chief Executive Officer, Capital Market Authority

Mr. Rober Blake, Senior Economist, World Bank

Mr. M.N. Kiwesi, Deputy Commissioner for Statistics, Uganda Bureau of Statistics

Mr. Kajubi, Ministry of Agriculture

Dr. William S. Kalema, Managing Director, Simba Blankets, Chairman, Uganda Investment Authority

Mr. James Nduati, Director of Operations, East African Development Bank

Mr. Stanley Mulumba, Managing Director, Ugarose Flowers Ltd

Mr. Charles Onyango-Obbo, Editor, *The Monitor Newspaper*

Mr. Anders Östman, Resident Representative, SIDA, Kampala

References

Ablo, E. and R. Reinikka (1998), "Do budgets really matter? Evidence from public spending on education and health in Uganda", Mimeo, World Bank, Washington DC.

African Development Bank (1998), *The African Development Report 1998*, ADB, Abidjan.

Appleton, S. (1998), "Changes in poverty in Uganda, 1992–1996", Mimeo, CSAE, Oxford University.

Bank of Uganda (1986), *Annual Report 1985*, Kampala.

— (1999), *Monthly Economic Report Jan–March*, Kampala.

— (various years), *Quarterly Bulletin of Statistics*, Kampala.

Berthélemy, J.-C. and L. Söderling (1998), "Contributions of TFP and capital accumulation to economic take-off: Some empirical evidence from Africa", Mimeo, OECD, Paris.

Berthélemy, J.-C. and A. Varoudakis (1996), "Policies for Economic Take-Off", Development Centre Policy Brief No 12, OECD, Development Assistance Committee.

Bevan, D. (1994), "Fiscal aspects of the transition from war to peace: With illustrations from Uganda and Ethiopia", WPS/94.7, CSAE, Oxford University.

Bigsten, A. (1993), "Regulations versus Price Reforms in Crisis Management. The Case of Kenya", in Blomström, M. and M. Lundahl (eds), *Economic Crisis in Africa: Perspectives on Policy Responses*, Routledge, London.

Bigsten, A., R. Aguilar, L. Hjalmarsson, G. Ikiara, A. Isaksson, P. Kimuyu, S. Kayizzi-Mugerwa, M. Manundu, W. Masai, N. Ndungu, S. Semboja and C. Wihlborg (1994), *Limitations and Rewards in Kenya's Manufacturing Sector: A Study of Enterprise Development*, World Bank, Washington DC.

Bigsten, A. et al. (1998), "Are there efficiency gains from exporting in African manufacturing?", Paper presented at an OECD conference in Johannesburg, November.

Bigsten, A. and S. Kayizzi-Mugerwa (1992), "Adaptation and Distress in the Urban Economy: A Study of Kampala Households", *World Development*, 20(10).

— (1999), *Crisis, Adjustment and Growth in Uganda. A Study of Adaptation in an African Economy*, Macmillan, London.

Bigsten, A. and K-O. Moene (1996), "Growth and Rent Dissipation: The Case of Kenya", *Journal of African Economies*, 5(2).

Botchwey, K., P. Collier, J.W. Gunning and K. Hamada (1998), "Report of the Group of Independent Persons Appointed to Conduct an Evaluation of Certain Aspects of the Enhanced Structural Adjustment Facility", Mimeo, IMF, Washington DC.

Burnside, C. and D. Dollar (1997), "Aid, Policy and Growth", Policy Research Working Paper No 1777, World Bank, Washington DC.

CIET International (1998), *Uganda National Integrity Survey, 1998*, Report submitted to the Inspectorate of Government, Kampala, August.

Collier, P. (1994), "Economic Aspects of the Ugandan Transition to Peace", in Azam, J.-P., D. Bevan, P. Collier, S. Dercon and J.W. Gunning (1994), *Some Economic Consequences of the Transition from Civil War to Peace*, Mimeo, CSAE, Oxford University.

— (1995), "The Marginalization of Africa", *International Labour Review*, 134:4–5.

— (1996), "A Commentary on the Ugandan economy: March 1996", Mimeo, CSAE, Oxford University.

— (1997), "Ugandan Trade Policy: Liberalisation in an environment of limited credibility", Mimeo, CSAE, Oxford University.

Collier, P. and J.W. Gunning (1995), "War, Peace and Private Portfolios", *World Development*, Vol. 23, No. 2.

Collins, C. and A. Green (1994), "Decentralisation and Primary Healthcare: Some Negative Implications in Developing Countries", *International Journal of Health Services*, Vol. 24, No. 2.

DAC (1996), "Shaping the 21st Century: The Contribution of Development Cooperation", OECD, Paris.

Devarajan, S., A.S. Rajkumar and V. Swaroop (1998), "What Does Aid Finance in Africa?", Mimeo, AERC.

Easterly, W. and R. Levine (1996), "Africa's Growth Tragedy: A Retrospective 1960–89", Policy Research Working Paper No 1503, World Bank, Washington DC.

Elbadawi, I. (1998), "External Aid: Help or Hindrance to Export Orientation in Africa?", Mimeo, AERC.

Elliott, C. (1973), "Employment and Income Distribution in Uganda", *Development Studies Discussion Paper*, No.1, University of East Anglia, Norwich.

Ewusi, K. (1973), "Changes in Distribution of Earnings of Africans in Recorded Employment in Uganda", *Economic Bulletin of Ghana*, 3(1).

Goetz, A.M. and R. Jenkins (1998), "Creating a Framework for Reducing Poverty: Institutional and Process Issues in National Poverty Policy—Uganda Country Report", Mimeo, IDS, Sussex, Birkbeck College, London.

Gray, C.W. (1996), "In Search of Owners: Privatisation and Corporate Governance in Transition Economies", *World Bank Research Observer*, 11(2).

Guillaumont, P., S. Guillaumont Jenneney and A. Varoudakis (1998), "Economic policy reform and growth prospects in emerging African economies", Technical paper, OECD Development Centre, Paris.

Henstridge, N.M. (1995), *Coffee and Money in Uganda: An Econometric Analysis*, Ph.D. Thesis, Exeter College, Oxford University.

Heyneman, S.P. (1979), "Why Impoverished Children Do Well in Ugandan Schools", *World Bank Reprint Series*, No. 111, World Bank.

Hirschman, A.O. (1958), *The Strategy of Economic Development*, Yale University Press, New Haven.

Hulten, C.R. and R.M. Schwab (1991), "Public Capital Formation and the Growth of Regional Manufacturing Industries", *National Tax Journal*, 44(4).

ILO (1997), *Adjustment, Employment and Labour Market Institutions in Sub-Saharan Africa: An Emerging Consensus on Consultative Policy Design?*, International Labour Office, Geneva.

Jamal, V. (1976), "Asians in Uganda, 1880–1972: Inequality and Expulsion", *Economic History Review*, Vol. 19, No. 4.

Kaheru, Z. (1990), "Health Cost Sharing Policy", *Policy Paper*, Ministry of Health, Entebbe.

Kanbur, R. (1998), "A Framework for Thinking through Reduced Aid Dependence in Africa", Mimeo, AERC.

Kasekende, L.A., P.K. Asea and A.C. Abuka (1998), "Trade Policy and Manufacturing Efficiency in a Liberalising Economy", Mimeo, Kampala.

Kasekende, L., D. Kitabire and M. Martin (1998), "Capital Inflows and Macroeconomic Policy in SSA", in Helleiner, G.K. (ed.), *Capital Account Regimes and the Developing Economies*, Macmillan, London.

Kasekende, L. and G. Ssemogerere (1994), "Exchange Rate Unification and Economic Development: The Case of Uganda 1987–92", *World Development*, 22(8).

Katumba, A.B. (1988), "The State of the Industrial Sector—1984", *Occasional Paper*, No. 6, Makerere Institute of Social Research.

Kayizzi-Mugerwa, S. (1993), "Urban Bustle/Rural Slumber: Dilemmas of Uneven Economic Recovery in Uganda", in Blomström, M. and M. Lundahl (eds), *Economic Crisis in Africa: Perspectives on Policy Responses*, Routledge, London.

— (1997), "Uganda 1996: Security, Credibility and Market Development", *Macroeconomic Report*, No.1, Sida, Stockholm.

— (1999a), *The African Economy, Policy, Institutions and the Future*, Routledge, London.

— (1999b), "Uganda at the End of the 1990s: A Medium-Term Assessment", Mimeo, Sida, Stockholm.

Kayizzi-Mugerwa, S. and A. Bigsten (1992), "On Structural Adjustment in Uganda", *Canadian Journal of Development Studies*, June.

Kisakye, J. (1996), "Political Background to Decentralisation, Democratic Decentralisation in Uganda: A New Approach to Local Government", in Villadsen, S. and F. Lubanga (eds), *Democratic Decentralisation in Uganda: A New Approach to Local Governance*, Fountain Publishers, Kampala.

Langseth, P. (1996), "Civil Service Reform: A General View", in Villadsen, S. and F. Lubanga (eds), *Democratic Decentralisation in Uganda: A New Approach to Local Governance*, Fountain Publishers, Kampala.

Langseth P. and J. Mugaju (eds) (1996), *Post-Conflict Uganda: Towards an Effective Civil Service*, Fountain Publishers, Kampala

Langseth, P., D. Pezullo, D. and F. Simpkin (1998), *Update: Uganda Efforts to Combat Corruption*, Report for Transparency International.

Local Finance Commission (1997), *Annual Report*, Kampala.

Malik, P. (1995), "The Central Bank, the Treasury and Monetary Autonomy—The Experience of Uganda", Annex 3.1, *African Development Report 1995*, African Development Bank, Abidjan.

Matovu, J.M. (1998a), "Labour Supply, Commodity Demand and Taxation of Households", Mimeo, CSAE, Oxford University.

— (1998b), *Fiscal Policies, Public Service Provision, and Human Productivity*, Dissertation, Oxford University, Oxford.

Mbire, B. (1997), *Exchange Rate Policy and Inflation: The Case of Uganda*, AERC Research Paper no 59, Nairobi.

Milner, C., O. Morrisey and N. Rudaheranwa (1998), "Protection, Trade Policy and Transport Costs: Effective Taxation of Ugandan Exporters", CREDIT Research Paper No 98/13, University of Nottingham.

Morrisey, O. and N. Rudaheranwa (1998), "Ugandan Trade Policy and Export Performance in the 1990s", CREDIT Research Paper No 98/12, University of Nottingham.

Museveni, Y. K. (1997), *Sowing the Mustard Seed*, McMillan, London

Mutalemwa, D., P. Noni and S. Wangwe (1998), "Managing the Transition from Aid Dependence: The Case of Tanzania", Mimeo, AERC.

Nsibambi, A. (1976), "The Politics of Education in Uganda", *The Uganda Journal*, Vol. 38.

Okurut, F.N., J.J.A.O. Odwee, and A. Adebua (1998), "Determinants of Regional Poverty in Uganda", Paper presented to the AERC bi-annual Workshop in Nairobi, December.

Odaet, C.F. (1990), "Implementing Education Policies in Uganda", *World Bank Discussion Papers*, No. 89, Washington, DC.

Opio-Odong, J.M.A. (1993), *Higher Education and Research in Uganda*, Acts Press, Nairobi and SAREC, Stockholm.

Oundo, G.B. and T. Burton (1992), "A Hungry Child Does Not Learn: Factors Affecting the Feeding of Children in Primary School, Kiyeyi Project Area, Tororo District", Report, Child Health Development Centre, Makerere University.

Private Sector Foundation (1996), *The Private Sector on Structural Adjustment Credit III*, Private Sector Foundation, Kampala.

Richaud, C. and A. Varoudakis (1999), "Securing Benefits from Globalisation: Progress Report on the Consistency between the Exchange Rate and Trade Policies in Africa", Mimeo, OECD Development Centre.

Robinson, D. (1990), "Civil Service Remuneration in Africa", *International Labour Review*, 129(3).

Rodrik, D. (1998), *Trade Policy and Economic Performance in Sub-Saharan Africa*, EGDI Report 1998:1, Swedish Ministry of Foreign Affairs, Stockholm.

Sachs, J.D. and A.M. Warner (1997), "Sources of Slow Growth in African Economies", *Journal of African Economies*, Vol. 6, No. 3, pp. 335–76.

Schiavo-Campo, S. (1996), "Reforming the Civil Service", *Finance and Development*, September.

Sekkat, K. and A. Varoudakis (1998), "Exchange Rate Management and Manufactured Exports in Sub-Saharan Africa", *Technical Paper*, No. 134, OECD Development Centre, March.

Semakula, V. (1996), "Rakai District in Development: Consequences of Decentralisation", in Villadsen, S. and F. Lubanga (eds), *Democratic Decentralisation in Uganda: A New Approach to Local Governance*, Fountain Publishers, Kampala.

Ssemogerere, G. and W.S. Kalema (1998), "Managing the Transition from Aid Dependency: Challenges and Opportunities for Uganda in the 21st Century", Mimeo, AERC.

Uganda (1965), *Background to the Budget 1965–66*, Ministry of Finance, Kampala.

— (1966), *Statistical Abstract 1965*, Statistics Division, Ministry of Planning and Economic Development, Kampala.

— (1967), *Statistical Abstract 1966*, Statistics Division, Ministry of Planning and Economic Development, Kampala.

— (1972), *Budget Speech*, Ministry of Finance, Kampala.

— (1977), *The Action Programme*, President's Office, Entebbe.

— (1981), *The Challenge of Recovery*, Communication from the Chair by A.M. Obote, Kampala.

— (1982), *The Report of the Public Service Salaries Review Commission 1981–82*, Government Printer, Entebbe.

— (1990), *Report of the Public Service Review and Re-Organisation Commission 1989–90*, Vol.1 Main Report, Ministry of Public Service, Kampala.

— (1990), *Statistical Bulletin No GDP/2 Gross Domestic Product of Uganda 1981–1989*, Ministry of Planning and Economic Development, Kampala

— (1993), *Report of an Independent Working Group on the Ugandan Economy*, President's Office, Kampala.

— (1996a), *Background to the Budget 1996/97*, Ministry of Finance and Economic Planning, Kampala.

— (1996b), *Demographic and Health Survey 1995*, Kampala.

— (1997a), *Public Service 2002*, Administrative Reform Secretariat, Ministry of Public Service, Kampala.

— (1997b), *Decentralisation in Uganda: Centre-Local Relations*, Decentralisation Secretariat, Ministry of Local Government, Kampala.

— (1997c), *Budget Speech*, Ministry of Finance, Kampala.

— (1997d), *Uganda Public Service Programme*, Ministry of Public Service, Kampala.

— (1997e), *Poverty Eradication Plan*, Ministry of Planning and Economic Development, Kampala.

— (1997f), *Poverty Trends in Uganda 1989–1995*, Ministry of Planning and Economic Development Discussion Paper No. 1, Co-ordination of Poverty Eradication Projects and the Department of Statistics, Kampala.

— (1998), *Budget Speech 1998/99*, Kampala

— (1998), *Statistical Abstract 1998*, Ministry of Planning and Economic Development, Kampala.

— (various years), *Uganda Statistical Bulletin*, Statistical Department, Entebbe.

— (various years), *Background to the Budget*, Ministry of Planning and Economic Development, Kampala.

— (various years), *Key Economic Indicators*, Ministry of Planning and Economic Development, Kampala.

Uganda Manufacturers Association (1995), *Proposals for the 1995/96 National Budget and Economic Policy: Going for Growth*, UMA, Kampala.

— (1998), *Manufacturer*, No.3., Kampala.

Uganda Investment Authority (1997), *Investor Survey Report*, Kampala.

— (1998), *Quarterly Report*, Kampala.

UNICEF (1994), "Children and Women in Uganda—a Situation Analysis", UNICEF, Kampala.

Van de Walle, N. (1998), "Managing Aid to Africa: The Rise and Decline of the Structural Adjustment Regime, Mimeo, AERC.

Van der Heijden, T. and J. Jitta (1993), "Economic Survival Strategies of Health Workers in Uganda", Study Report, Child Health and Development Centre, Makerere University.

Villadsen, S. and F. Lubanga (eds) (1996), *Democratic Decentralisation in Uganda: A New Approach to Local Governance*, Fountain Publishers, Kampala

Wade, R. (1985), "The Market for Public Office: Why the Indian State is Not Better at Development", *World Development*, 13(4).

White, H. (1999), "Aid and Economic Reform", in Kayizzi-Mugerwa, S. (ed.), *The African Economy, Policies, Institutions and the Future*, Routledge, London.

Wood, A. (1994), *North-South Trade, Employment and Inequality: Changing fortunes in a skill-driven world*, Clarendon Press, Oxford.

World Bank (1982), *Country Economic Memorandum*, Washington DC.

World Bank (1988), *Uganda—towards stabilisation and Economic Recovery*, Washington DC.

— (1995), "Uganda: The challenge of growth and poverty reduction", Washington, DC.

— (1997), *Republic of Uganda: Third Structural Adjustment Credit Project*, Washington DC.

— (1998a), "Report and Recommendation of the President of the International Development Association to the Executive Directors on Assistance to the Republic of Uganda under the Debt Initiative Completion Project Document", March 20, Washington DC.

— (1998b), "Memorandum of the President of the International Development Association to the Executive Directors on a Country Assistance Strategy of the World Bank Group for the Republic of Uganda", April 30, Washington DC.

— (1998c), "Report and Recommendation of the Managing Director of the International Development Association to the Executive Directors on a proposed interim fund credit in an amount of SDR 91.1 million to the Republic of Uganda for a third structural adjustment credit project", May 1, Washington DC.

Research Reports published by the Institute

Some of the reports are out of print. Photocopies of these reports can be obtained at a cost of SEK 0:50/page.

1. Meyer-Heiselberg, Richard, *Notes from Liberated African Department in the Archives at Fourah Bay College, Freetown, Sierra Leone.* 61 pp. 1967 (OUT-OF-PRINT)

2. Not published.

3. Carlsson, Gunnar, *Benthonic Fauna in African Watercourses with Special Reference to Black Fly Populations.* 13 pp. 1968 (OUT-OF-PRINT)

4. Eldblom, Lars, *Land Tenure—Social Organization and Structure.* 18 pp. 1969 (OUT-OF-PRINT)

5. Bjerén, Gunilla, *Makelle Elementary School Drop-Out. 1967.* 80 pp. 1969 (OUT-OF-PRINT)

6. Møberg, Jens Peter, *Report Concerning the Soil Profile Investigation and Collection of Soil Samples in the West Lake Region of Tanzania.* 44 pp. 1970 (OUT-OF-PRINT)

7. Selinus, Ruth, *The Traditional Foods of the Central Ethiopian Highlands.* 34 pp. 1971 (OUT-OF-PRINT)

8. Hägg, Ingemund, *Some State-Controlled Industrial Companies in Tanzania. A Case Study.* 18 pp. 1971 (OUT-OF-PRINT)

9. Bjerén, Gunilla, *Some Theoretical and Methodological Aspects of the Study of African Urbanization.* 38 pp. 1971 (OUT-OF-PRINT)

10. Linné, Olga, *An Evaluation of Kenya Science Teacher's College.* 67 pp. 1971. SEK 45,-

11. Nellis, John R., *Who Pays Tax in Kenya?* 22 pp. 1972. SEK 45,-

12. Bondestam, Lars, *Population Growth Control in Kenya.* 59 pp. 1972 (OUT OF PRINT)

13. Hall, Budd L., *Wakati Wa Furaha. An Evaluation of a Radio Study Group Campaign.* 47 pp. 1973. SEK 45,-

14. Ståhl, Michael, *Contradictions in Agricultural Development. A Study of Three Minimum Package Projects in Southern Ethiopia.* 65 pp. 1973 (OUT-OF-PRINT)

15. Linné, Olga, *An Evaluation of Kenya Science Teachers College. Phase II 1970–71.* 91 pp. 1973 (OUT-OF-PRINT)

16. Lodhi, Abdulaziz Y., *The Institution of Slavery in Zanzibar and Pemba.* 40 pp. 1973. ISBN 91-7106-066-9 (OUT-OF-PRINT)

17. Lundqvist, Jan, *The Economic Structure of Morogoro Town. Some Sectoral and Regional Characteristics of a Medium-Sized African Town.* 70 pp. 1973. ISBN 91-7106-068-5 (OUT-OF-PRINT)

18. Bondestam, Lars, *Some Notes on African Statistics. Collection, Reliability and Interpretation.* 59 pp. 1973. ISBN 91-7106-069-4 (OUT-OF-PRINT)

19. Jensen, Peter Føge, *Soviet Research on Africa. With Special Reference to International Relations.* 68 pp. 1973. ISBN 91-7106-070-7 (OUT-OF-PRINT)

20. Sjöström, Rolf & Margareta, *YDLC—A Literacy Campaign in Ethiopia. An Introductory Study and a Plan for Further Research.* 72 pp. 1973. ISBN 91-7106-071-5 (OUT-OF-PRINT)

21. Ndongko, Wilfred A., *Regional Economic Planning in Cameroon.* 21 pp. 1974. SEK 45,-. ISBN 91-7106-073-1

22. Pipping-van Hulten, Ida, *An Episode of Colonial History: The German Press in Tanzania 1901–1914.* 47 pp. 1974. SEK 45,-. ISBN 91-7106-077-4

23. Magnusson, Åke, *Swedish Investments in South Africa.* 57 pp. 1974. SEK 45,-. ISBN 91-7106-078-2

24. Nellis, John R., *The Ethnic Composition of Leading Kenyan Government Positions.* 26 pp. 1974. SEK 45,-. ISBN 91-7106-079-0

25. Francke, Anita, *Kibaha Farmers' Training Centre. Impact Study 1965–1968.* 106 pp. 1974. SEK 45,-. ISBN 91-7106-081-2

26. Aasland, Tertit, *On the Move-to-the-Left in Uganda 1969–1971.* 71 pp. 1974. SEK 45,-. ISBN 91-7106-083-9

27. Kirk-Greene, Anthony H.M., *The Genesis of the Nigerian Civil War and the Theory of Fear.* 32 pp. 1975. SEK 45,-. ISBN 91-7106-085-5

28. Okereke, Okoro, *Agrarian Development Pro grammes of African Countries. A Reappraisal of Problems of Policy.* 20 pp. 1975. SEK 45,-. ISBN 91-7106-086-3

29. Kjekshus, Helge, *The Elected Elite. A Socio-Economic Profile of Candidates in Tanzania's Parliamentary Election, 1970.* 40 pp. 1975. SEK 45,-. ISBN 91-7106-087-1

30. Frantz, Charles, *Pastoral Societies, Stratification and National Integration in Africa.* 34 pp. 1975. ISBN 91-7106-088-X (OUT OF PRINT)

31. Esh, Tina & Illith Rosenblum, *Tourism in Developing Countries—Trick or Treat? A Report from the Gambia.* 80 pp. 1975. ISBN 91-7106-094-4 (OUT-OF-PRINT)

32. Clayton, Anthony, *The 1948 Zanzibar General Strike.* 66 pp. 1976. ISBN 91-7106-094-4 (OUT OF PRINT)

33. Pipping, Knut, *Land Holding in the Usangu Plain. A Survey of Two Villages in the Southern Highlands of Tanzania.* 122 pp. 1976. ISBN 91-7106-097-9 (OUT OF PRINT)

34. Lundström, Karl Johan, *North-Eastern Ethiopia: Society in Famine. A Study of Three Social Institutions in a Period of Severe Strain.* 80 pp. 1976. ISBN 91-7106-098-7 (OUT-OF-PRINT)

35. Magnusson, Åke, *The Voice of South Africa*. 55 pp. 1976. ISBN 91-7106-106-1 (OUT OF PRINT)

36. Ghai, Yash P., *Reflection on Law and Economic Integration in East Africa*. 41 pp. 1976. ISBN 91-7106-105-3 (OUT-OF-PRINT)

37. Carlsson, Jerker, *Transnational Companies in Liberia. The Role of Transnational Companies in the Economic Development of Liberia*. 51 pp. 1977. SEK 45,-. ISBN 91-7106-107-X

38. Green, Reginald H., *Toward Socialism and Self Reliance. Tanzania's Striving for Sustained Transition Projected*. 57 pp. 1977. ISBN 91-7106-108-8 (OUT-OF-PRINT)

39. Sjöström, Rolf & Margareta, *Literacy Schools in a Rural Society. A Study of Yemissrach Dimts Literacy Campaign in Ethiopia*. 130 pp. 1977. ISBN 91-7106-109-6 (OUT-OF-PRINT)

40. Ståhl, Michael, *New Seeds in Old Soil. A Study of the Land Reform Process in Western Wollega, Ethiopia 1975–76*. 90 pp. 1977. SEK 45,-. ISBN 91-7106-112-6

41. Holmberg, Johan, *Grain Marketing and Land Reform in Ethiopia. An Analysis of the Marketing and Pricing of Food Grains in 1976 after the Land Reform*. 34 pp. 1977. ISBN 91-7106-113-4 (OUT-OF-PRINT)

42. Egerö, Bertil, *Mozambique and Angola: Reconstruction in the Social Sciences*. 78 pp. 1977. ISBN 91-7106-118-5 (OUT OF PRINT)

43. Hansen, H. B., *Ethnicity and Military Rule in Uganda*. 136 pp. 1977. ISBN 91-7106-118-5 (OUT-OF-PRINT)

44. Bhagavan, M.R., *Zambia: Impact of Industrial Strategy on Regional Imbalance and Social Inequality*. 76 pp. 1978. ISBN 91-7106-119-3 (OUT OF PRINT)

45. Aaby, Peter, *The State of Guinea-Bissau. African Socialism or Socialism in Africa?* 35 pp. 1978. ISBN 91-7106-133-9 (OUT-OF-PRINT)

46. Abdel-Rahim, Muddathir, *Changing Patterns of Civilian-Military Relations in the Sudan*. 32 pp. 1978. ISBN 91-7106-137-1 (OUT-OF-PRINT)

47. Jönsson, Lars, *La Révolution Agraire en Algérie. Historique, contenu et problèmes*. 84 pp. 1978. ISBN 91-7106-145-2 (OUT-OF-PRINT)

48. Bhagavan, M.R., *A Critique of "Appropriate" Technology for Underdeveloped Countries*. 56 pp. 1979. SEK 45,-. ISBN 91-7106-150-9

49. Bhagavan, M.R., *Inter-Relations Between Technological Choices and Industrial Strategies in Third World Countries*. 79 pp. 1979. SEK 45,-. ISBN 91-7106-151-7

50. Torp, Jens Erik, *Industrial Planning and Development in Mozambique. Some Preliminary Considerations*. 59 pp. 1979. ISBN 91-7106-153-3 (OUT-OF-PRINT)

51. Brandström, Per, Jan Hultin & Jan Lindström, *Aspects of Agro-Pastoralism in East Africa*. 60 pp. 1979. ISBN 91-7106-155-X (OUT OF PRINT)

52. Egerö, Bertil, *Colonization and Migration. A Summary of Border-Crossing Movements in Tanzania before 1967*. 45 pp. 1979. SEK 45,-. ISBN 91-7106-159-2

53. Simson, Howard, *Zimbabwe—A Country Study*. 138 pp. 1979. ISBN 91-7106-160-6 (OUT-OF-PRINT)

54. Beshir, Mohamed Omer, *Diversity Regionalism and National Unity*. 50 pp. 1979. ISBN 91-7106-166-5 (OUT-OF-PRINT)

55. Eriksen, Tore Linné, *Modern African History: Some Historiographical Observations*. 27 pp. 1979. ISBN 91-7106-167-3 (OUT OF PRINT)

56. Melander, Göran, *Refugees in Somalia*. 48 pp. 1980. SEK 45,-. ISBN 91-7106-169-X

57. Bhagavan, M.R., *Angola: Prospects for Socialist Industrialisation*. 48 pp. 1980. ISBN 91-7106-175-4 (OUT OF PRINT)

58. Green, Reginald H., *From Südwestafrika to Namibia. The Political Economy of Transition*. 45 pp. 1981. SEK 45,-. ISBN 91-7106-188-6

59. Isaksen, Jan, *Macro-Economic Management and Bureaucracy: The Case of Botswana*. 53 pp. 1981. SEK 45,-. ISBN 91-7106-192-4

60. Odén, Bertil, *The Macroeconomic Position of Botswana*. 84 pp. 1981. SEK 45,-. ISBN 91-7106-193-2

61. Westerlund, David, *From Socialism to Islam? Notes on Islam as a Political Factor in Contemporary Africa*. 62 pp. 1982. SEK 45,-. ISBN 91-7106-203-3

62. Tostensen, Arne, *Dependence and Collective Self-Reliance in Southern Africa. The Case of the Southern African Development Coordination Conference (SADCC)*. 170 pp. 1982. ISBN 91-7106-207-6 (OUT-OF-PRINT)

63. Rudebeck, Lars, *Problèmes de pouvoir populaire et de développement. Transition difficile en Guinée-Bissau*. 73 pp. 1982. ISBN 91-7106-208-4 (OUT-OF-PRINT)

64. Nobel, Peter, *Refugee Law in the Sudan. With The Refugee Conventions and The Regulation of Asylum Act of 1974*. 56 pp. 1982. SEK 45,-. ISBN 91-7106-209-2

65. Sano, H-O, *The Political Economy of Food in Nigeria 1960–1982. A Discussion on Peasants, State, and World Economy*. 108 pp. 1983. ISBN 91-7106-210-6 (OUT-OF-PRINT)

66. Kjærby, Finn, *Problems and Contradictions in the Development of Ox-Cultivation in Tanzania*. 164 pp. 1983. SEK 60,-. ISBN 91-7106-211-4

67. Kibreab, Gaim, *Reflections on the African Refugee Problem: A Critical Analysis of Some Basic Assumptions*. 154 pp. 1983. ISBN 91-7106-212-2 (OUT-OF-PRINT) (

68. Haarløv, Jens, *Labour Regulation and Black Workers' Struggles in South Africa*. 80 pp. 1983. SEK 20,-. ISBN 91-7106-213-0

69. Matshazi, Meshack Jongilanga & Christina Tillfors, *A Survey of Workers' Education Activities in Zimbabwe, 1980–1981*. 85 pp. 1983. SEK 45,-. ISBN 91-7106-217-3

70. Hedlund, Hans & Mats Lundahl, *Migration and Social Change in Rural Zambia*. 107 pp. 1983. SEK 50,-. ISBN 91-7106-220-3

71. Gasarasi, Charles P., *The Tripartite Approach to the Resettlement and Integration of Rural Refugees in Tanzania*. 76 pp. 1984. SEK 45,-. ISBN 91-7106-222-X

72. Kameir, El-Wathig & I. Kursany, *Corruption as a "Fifth" Factor of Production in the Sudan*. 33 pp. 1985. SEK 45,-. ISBN 91-7106-223-8

73. Davies, Robert, *South African Strategy Towards Mozambique in the Post-Nkomati Period. A Critical Analysis of Effects and Implications*. 71 pp. 1985. SEK 45,-. ISBN 91-7106-238-6

74. Bhagavan, M.R. *The Energy Sector in SADCC Countries. Policies, Priorities and Options in the Context of the African Crisis*. 41 pp. 1985. SEK 45,-. ISBN 91-7106-240-8

75. Bhagavan, M.R. *Angola's Political Economy 1975–1985*. 89 pp. 1986. SEK 45,-. ISBN 91-7106-248-3

76. Östberg, Wilhelm, *The Kondoa Transformation. Coming to Ggrips with Soil Erosion in Central Tanzania*. 99 pp. 1986. ISBN 91-7106-251-3 (OUT OF PRINT)

77. Fadahunsi, Akin, *The Development Process and Technology. A Case for a Resources Based Development Strategy in Nigeria*. 41 pp. 1986. SEK 45,-. ISBN 91-7106-265-3

78. Suliman, Hassan Sayed, *The Nationalist Movements in the Maghrib. A Comparative Approach*. 87 pp. 1987. SEK 45,-. ISBN 91-7106-266-1

79. Saasa, Oliver S., *Zambia's Policies towards Foreign Investment. The Case of the Mining and Non-Mining Sectors*. 65 pp. 1987. SEK 45,-. ISBN 91-7106-271-8

80. Andræ, Gunilla & Björn Beckman, *Industry Goes Farming. The Nigerian Raw Material Crisis and the Case of Textiles and Cotton*. 68 pp. 1987. SEK 50,-. ISBN 91-7106-273-4

81. Lopes, Carlos & Lars Rudebeck, *The Socialist Ideal in Africa. A Debate*. 27 pp. 1988. SEK 45,-. ISBN 91-7106-280-7

82. Hermele, Kenneth, *Land Struggles and Social Differentiation in Southern Mozambique. A Case Study of Chokwe, Limpopo 1950–1987*. 64 pp. 1988. SEK 50,- ISBN 91-7106-282-3

83. Smith, Charles David, *Did Colonialism Capture the Peasantry? A Case Study of the Kagera District, Tanza nia*. 34 pp. 1989. SEK 45,-. ISBN 91-7106-289-0

84. Hedlund, S. & M. Lundahl, *Ideology as a Deter minant of Economic Systems: Nyerere and Ujamaa in Tanzania*. 54 pp. 1989. SEK 50,-. ISBN 91-7106-291-2

85. Lindskog, Per & Jan Lundqvist, *Why Poor Children Stay Sick. The Human Ecology of Child Health and Welfare in Rural Malawi*. 111 pp. 1989. SEK 60,-. ISBN 91-7106-284-X

86. Holmén, Hans, *State, Cooperatives and Develop ment in Africa*. 87 pp. 1990. SEK 60,-. ISBN 91-7106-300-5

87. Zetterqvist, Jenny, *Refugees in Botswana in the Light of International Law*. 83 pp. 1990. SEK 60,-. ISBN 91-7106-304-8

88. Rwelamira, Medard, *Refugees in a Chess Game: Reflections on Botswana, Lesotho and Swaziland Refugee Policies*. 63 pp. 1990. SEK 60,-. ISBN 91-7106-306-4

89. Gefu, Jerome O., *Pastoralist Perspectives in Nigeria. The Fulbe of Udubo Grazing Reserve*. 106 pp. 1992. SEK 60,-. ISBN 91-7106-324-2

90. Heino, Timo-Erki, *Politics on Paper. Finland's South Africa Policy 1945–1991*. 121 pp. 1992. SEK 60,-. ISBN 91-7106-326-9

91. Eriksson, Gun, *Peasant Response to Price Incentives in Tanzania. A Theoretical and Empirical Investigation*. 84 pp. 1993. SEK 60,- . ISBN 91-7106-334-X

92. Chachage, C.S.L., Magnus Ericsson & Peter Gibbon, *Mining and Structural Adjustment. Studies on Zimbabwe and Tanzania*. 107 pp. 1993. SEK 60,-. ISBN 91-7106-340-4

93. Neocosmos, Michael, *The Agrarian Question in Southern Africa and "Accumulation from Below". Economics and Politics in the Struggle for Democracy*. 79 pp. 1993. SEK 60,-. ISBN 91-7106-342-0

94. Vaa, Mariken, *Towards More Appropriate Technologies? Experiences from the Water and Sanitation Sector*. 91 pp. 1993. SEK 60,-. ISBN 91-7106-343-9

95. Kanyinga, Karuti, Andrew Kiondo & Per Tidemand, *The New Local Level Politics in East Africa. Studies on Uganda, Tanzania and Kenya*. 119 pp. 1994. SEK 60,-. ISBN 91-7106-348-X

96. Odén, Bertil, H. Melber, T. Sellström & C. Tapscott. *Namibia and External Resources. The Case of Swedish Development Assistance*. 122 pp. 1994. SEK 60,-. ISBN 91-7106-351-X

97. Moritz, Lena, *Trade and Industrial Policies in the New South Africa*. 61 pp. 1994. SEK 60,-. ISBN 91-7106-355-2

98. Osaghae, Eghosa E., *Structural Adjustment and Ethnicity in Nigeria*. 66 pp. 1995. SEK 60,-. ISBN 91-7106-373-0

99. Soiri, Iina, *The Radical Motherhood. Namibian Women's Independence Struggle*. 115 pp. 1996. SEK 60,-. ISBN 91-7106-380-3.

100. Rwebangira, Magdalena K., *The Legal Status of Women and Poverty in Tanzania*. 58 pp. 1996. SEK 60,-. ISBN 91-7106-391-9

101. Bijlmakers, Leon A., Mary T. Bassett & David M. Sanders, *Health and Structural Adjustment in Rural and Urban Zimbabwe*. 78 pp. 1996. SEK 60,-. ISBN 91-7106-393-5

102. Gibbon, Peter & Adebayo O. Olukoshi, *Structural Adjustment and Socio-Economic Change in Sub-Saharan Africa. Some Conceptual, Methodological and Research Issues*. 101 pp. 1996. SEK 80,-. ISBN 91-7106-397-8

103. Egwu, Samuel G., *Structural Adjustment, Agrarian Change and Rural Ethnicity in Nigeria*. 124 pp. 1998. SEK 80,-. ISBN 91-7106-426-5

104. Olukoshi, Adebayo O., *The Elusive Prince of Denmark. Structural Adjustment and the Crisis of Governance in Africa*. 59 pp. 1998. SEK 80,-. ISBN 91-7106-428-1

105. Bijlmakers, Leon A., Mary T. Bassett & David M. Sanders, *Socioeconomic Stress, Health and Child Nutritional Status in Zimbabwe at a Time*

of Economic Structural Adjustment. A Three Year Longitudinal Study. 127 pp. 1998. SEK 80,-. ISBN 91-7106-434-6

106. Mupedziswa, Rodrick and Perpetua Gumbo, *Structural Adjustment and Women Informal Sector Traders in Harare, Zimbabwe.* 123 pp. 1998. SEK 80,-. ISBN 917106-435-4

107. Chiwele, D.K., P. Muyatwa-Sipula and H. Kalinda, *Private Sector Response to Agricultural Marketing Liberalisation in Zambia. A Case Study of Eastern Provice Maize Markets.* 90 pp. SEK 80,-. ISBN 91-7106-436-2

108. Amanor, K.S., *Global Restructuring and Land Rights in Ghana. Forest Food Chains, Timber and Rural Livelihoods.* 154 pp. 1999. SEK 80,-. ISBN 91-7106-437-0

109. Ongile, G.A., *Gender and Agricultural Supply Responses to Structural Adjustment Programmes. A Case Study of Smallholder Tea Producers in Kericho, Kenya.* 91 pp. 1999. SEK 80,- ISBN 91-7106-440-0

110. Sachikonye, Lloyd M., *Restructuring or De-Industrializing? Zimbabwe's Textile and Metal Industries under Structural Adjustment.* 107 pp. 1999. SEK 100,-. ISBN 91-7106-444-3

111. Gaidzanwa, Rudo, *Voting with their Feet. Migrant Zimbabwean Nurses and Doctors in the Era of Structural Adjustment.* 84 pp. 1999. SEK 100,-. ISBN 91-7106-445-1

112. Andersson, Per-Åke, Arne Bigsten and Håkan Persson, *Foreign Aid, Debt and Growth in Zambia.* 133 pp. 2000. SEK 100,-. ISBN 91-7106-462-1

113. Hashim, Yahaya and Kate Meagher, *Cross-Border Trade and the Parallel Currency Market —Trade and Finance in the Context of Structural Adjustment. A Case Study from Kano, Nigeria.* 118 pp. 1999. SEK 100,-. ISBN 91-7106-449-4

114. Schlyter, Ann, *Recycled Inequalitites. Youth and gender in George compound, Zambia,* 135 pp. 1999. SEK 100,-. ISBN 91-7106-455-9

115. Kanyinga, Karuti, *Re-Distribution from Above. The Politics of Land Rights and Squatting in Coastal Kenya.* 126 pp. 2000. SEK 100,-. ISBN 91-7106-464-8

116. Amanor, Kojo Sebastian, *Land, Labour and the Family in Southern Ghana. A Critique of Land Policy under Neo-Liberalisation.* 127 pp. 2001. SEK 100,-. ISBN 91-7106-468-0

117. Mupedziswa, Rodreck and Perpetua Gumbo, *Women Informal Traders in Harare and the Struggle for Survival in an Environment of Economic Reforms.* 118 pp. 2001. SEK 100,-. ISBN 91-7106-469-9

118. Bigsten, Arne and Steve Kayizzi-Mugerwa, *Is Uganda an Emerging Economy? A report for the OECD project "Emerging Africa".* 105 pp. 2001. SEK 100,-. ISBN 91-7106-470-2